Historic  Hunters

By

H. Addington Bruce

Echo Library 2009

Published by

Echo Library
131 High St.
Teddington
Middlesex TW11 8HH

ISBN 978-1-4068-2886-3

HISTORIC GHOSTS AND GHOST HUNTERS

BY

H. ADDINGTON BRUCE

Author of "The Riddle of Personality"

NEW YORK
MOFFAT, YARD & COMPANY
1908

Published, September, 1908
The Plimpton Press Norwood Mass. U.S.A.

To
THE MEMORY OF MY FRIEND
JOHN J. HENRY

CONTENTS

PREFACE

The following pages represent in the main a discussion of certain celebrated mysteries, as viewed in the light of the discoveries set forth in the writer's earlier work "The Riddle of Personality."

That dealt, it may briefly be recalled, with the achievements of those scientists whose special endeavor it is to illumine the nature of human personality. On the one hand, it reviewed the work of the psychopathologists, or investigators of abnormal mental life; and, on the other hand, the labors of the psychical researchers, those enthusiastic and patient explorers of the seemingly supernormal in human experience. Emphasis was laid on the fact that the two lines of inquiry are more closely interrelated than is commonly supposed, and that the discoveries made in each aid in the solution of problems apparently belonging exclusively in the other.

To this phase of the subject the writer now returns. The problems under examination are, all of them, problems in psychical research: yet, as will be found, the majority in no small measure depend for elucidation on facts brought to light by the psychopathologists. Of course, it is not claimed that the last word has here been said with respect to any one of these human enigmas. But it is believed that, thanks to the knowledge gained by the investigations of the past quarter of a century, approximately correct solutions have been reached; and that, in any event, it is by no means imperative to regard the phenomena in question as inexplicable, or as explicable only on a spiritistic basis.

Before attempting to solve the problems, it manifestly was necessary to state them. In doing this the writer has sought to present them in a readable and attractive form, but without any distortion or omission of material facts.

H. ADDINGTON BRUCE.

BROOKLINE, N. H., July, 1908.

I

The Devils of Loudun

Loudun is a small town in France about midway between the ancient and romantic cities of Tours and Poitiers. To-day it is an exceedingly unpretentious and an exceedingly sleepy place; but in the seventeenth century it was in vastly better estate. Then its markets, its shops, its inns, lacked not business. Its churches were thronged with worshipers. Through its narrow streets proud noble and prouder ecclesiastic, thrifty merchant and active artisan, passed and repassed in an unceasing stream. It was rich in points of interest, preëminent among which were its castle and its convent. In the castle the stout-hearted Loudunians found a refuge and a stronghold against the ambitions of the feudal lords and the tyranny of the crown. To its convent, pleasantly situated in a grove of time-honored trees, they sent their children to be educated.

It is to the convent that we must turn our steps; for it was from the convent that the devils were let loose to plague the good people of Loudun. And in order to understand the course of events, we must first make ourselves acquainted with its history. Very briefly, then, it, like many other institutions of its kind, was a product of the Catholic counter-reformation designed to stem the rising tide of Protestantism. It came into being in 1616, and was of the Ursuline order, which had been introduced into France not many years earlier. From the first it proved a magnet for the daughters of the nobility, and soon boasted a goodly complement of nuns.

At their head, as mother superior, was a certain Jeanne de Belfiel, of noble birth and many attractive qualities, but with characteristics which, as the sequel will show, wrought much woe to others as well as to the poor gentlewoman herself. Whatever her defects, however, she labored tirelessly in the interests of the convent, and in this respect was ably seconded by its father confessor, worthy Father Moussaut, a man of rare good sense and possessing a firm hold on the consciences and affections of the nuns.

Conceive their grief, therefore, when he suddenly sickened and died. Now ensued an anxious time pending the appointment of his successor. Two names were foremost for consideration—that of Jean Mignon, chief canon of the Church of the Holy Cross, and that of Urbain Grandier, curé of Saint Peter's of Loudun. Mignon was a zealous and learned ecclesiastic, but belied his name by being cold, suspicious, and, some would have it, unscrupulous. Grandier, on the contrary, was frank and ardent and generous, and was idolized by the people of Loudun. But he had serious failings. He was most unclerically gallant, was tactless, was overready to take offense, and, his wrath once fully roused, was unrelenting. Accordingly, little surprise was felt when the choice ultimately fell, not on him but on Mignon.

With Mignon the devils entered the Ursuline convent. Hardly had he been installed when rumors began to go about of strange doings within its quiet walls;

and that there was something in these rumors became evident on the night of October 12, 1632, when two magistrates of Loudun, the bailie and the civil lieutenant, were hurriedly summoned to the convent to listen to an astonishing story. For upwards of a fortnight, it appeared, several of the nuns, including Mother Superior Belfiel, had been tormented by specters and frightful visions. Latterly they had given every evidence of being possessed by evil spirits. With the assistance of another priest, Father Barré, Mignon had succeeded in exorcising the demons out of all the afflicted save the mother superior and a Sister Claire.

In their case every formula known to the ritual had failed. The only conclusion was that they were not merely possessed but bewitched, and much as he disliked to bring notoriety on the convent, the father confessor had decided it was high time to learn who was responsible for the dire visitation. He had called the magistrates, he explained, in order that legal steps might be taken to apprehend the wizard, it being well established that "devils when duly exorcised must speak the truth," and that consequently there could be no doubt as to the identity of the offender, should the evil spirits be induced to name the source of their authority.

Without giving the officials time to recover from their amazement, Mignon led them to an upper room, where they found the mother superior and Sister Claire, wan-faced and fragile looking creatures on whose countenances were expressions of fear that would have inspired pity in the most stony-hearted. About them hovered monks and nuns. At sight of the strangers, Sister Claire lapsed into a semi-comatose condition; but the mother superior uttered piercing shrieks, and was attacked by violent convulsions that lasted until the father confessor spoke to her in a commanding tone. Then followed a startling dialogue, carried on in Latin between Mignon and the soi-disant demon possessing her.

"Why have you entered this maiden's body?"

"Because of hatred."

"What sign do you bring?"

"Flowers."

"What flowers?"

"Roses."

"Who has sent them?"

A moment's hesitation, then the single word—"Urbain."

"Tell us his surname?"

"Grandier."

In an instant the room was in an uproar. But the magistrates did not lose their heads. To the bailie in especial the affair had a suspicious look. He had heard the devil "speak worse Latin than a boy of the fourth class," he had noted the mother superior's hesitancy in pronouncing Grandier's name, and he was well aware that deadly enmity had long existed between Grandier and Mignon. So he placed little faith in the latter's protestation that the naming of his rival had taken him completely by surprise. Consulting with his colleague, he coldly informed Mignon that before any arrest could be made there must be further investigation, and, promising to return next day, bade them good night.

Next day found the convent besieged by townspeople, indignant at the accusation against the popular priest, and determined to laugh the devils out of existence. Grandier himself, burning with rage, hastened to the bailie and demanded that the nuns be separately interrogated, and by other inquisitors than Mignon and Barré. In these demands the bailie properly acquiesced; but, on attempting in person to enforce his orders to that effect, he was denied admittance to the convent. Excitement ran high; so high that, fearful for his personal safety, Mignon consented to accept as exorcists two priests appointed, not by the bailie, but by the Bishop of Poitiers—who, it might incidentally be mentioned, had his own reasons for disliking Grandier.

Exorcising now went on daily, to the disgust of the serious-minded, the mystification of the incredulous, the delight of sensation-mongers, and the baffled fury of Grandier. So far the play, if melodramatic, had not approached the tragic. Sometimes it degenerated to the broadest farce comedy. Thus, on one occasion when the devil was being read out of the mother superior, a crashing sound was heard and a huge black cat tumbled down the chimney and scampered about the room. At once the cry was raised that the devil had taken the form of a cat, a mad chase ensued, and it would have gone hard with pussy had not a nun chanced to recognize in it the pet of the convent.

Still, there were circumstances which tended to inspire conviction in the mind of many. The convulsions of the possessed were undoubtedly genuine, and undoubtedly they manifested phenomena seemingly inexplicable on any naturalistic basis. A contemporary writer, describing events of a few months later, when several recruits had been added to their ranks, states that some "when comatose became supple like a thin piece of lead, so that their body could be bent in every direction, forward, backward, or sideways, till their head touched the ground," and that others showed no sign of pain when struck, pinched, or pricked. Then, too, they whirled and danced and grimaced and howled in a manner impossible to any one in a perfectly normal state.

For a few brief weeks Grandier enjoyed a respite, thanks to the intervention of his friend, the Archbishop of Bordeaux, who threatened to send a physician and priests of his own choice to examine the possessed, a threat of itself sufficient, apparently, to put the devils to flight. But they returned with undiminished vigor upon the arrival in Loudun of a powerful state official who, unfortunately for Grandier, was a relative of Mother Superior Belfiel's. This official, whose name was Laubardemont, had come to Loudun on a singular mission. Richelieu, the celebrated cardinal statesman, in the pursuit of his policy of strengthening the crown and weakening the nobility, had resolved to level to the ground the fortresses and castles of interior France, and among those marked for destruction was the castle of Loudun. Thither, therefore, he dispatched Laubardemont to see that his orders were faithfully executed.

Naturally, the cardinal's commissioner became interested in the trouble that had befallen his kinswoman, and the more interested when Mignon hinted to him that there was reason to believe that the suspected wizard was also the author of a recent satire which had set the entire court laughing at Richelieu's expense. What lent plausibility to this charge was the fact that the satire had been universally accredited to a court beauty formerly one of Grandier's parishioners. Also there was the fact that in days gone by, when Richelieu was merely a deacon, he had had a violent quarrel with Grandier over a question of precedence. Putting two and two together, and knowing that it would result to his own advantage to unearth the real author to the satire, Laubardemont turned a willing ear to the suggestion that the woman in question had allowed her old pastor to shield himself behind her name.

Back to Paris the commissioner galloped to carry the story to Richelieu. The cardinal's anger knew no bounds. From the King he secured a warrant for Grandier's arrest, and to this he added a decree investing Laubardemont with full inquisitorial powers. Events now moved rapidly. Though forewarned by Parisian friends, Grandier refused to seek safety by flight, and was arrested in spectacular fashion while on his way to say mass. His home was searched, his papers were seized, and he himself was thrown into an improvised dungeon in a house belonging to Mignon. Witnesses in his favor were intimidated, while those willing to testify against him were liberally rewarded. To such lengths did the prosecution go that, discovering a strong undercurrent of popular indignation, Laubardemont actually procured from the King and council a decree prohibiting any appeal from his decisions, and gave out that, since King and cardinal believed in the enchantment, any one denying it would be held guilty of lese majesty divine and human.

Under these circumstances Grandier was doomed from the outset. But he made a desperate struggle, and his opponents were driven to sore straits to bolster up their case. The devils persisted in speaking bad Latin, and continually failed to meet tests which they themselves had suggested. Sometimes their failures were only too plainly the result of human intervention.

For instance, the mother superior's devil promised that, on a given night and in the church of the Holy Cross, he would lift Laubardemont's cap from his head and keep it suspended in mid-air while the commissioner intoned a *miserere*. When the time came for the fulfilment of this promise two of the spectators noticed that Laubardemont had taken care to seat himself at a goodly distance from the other participants. Quietly leaving the church, these amateur detectives made their way to the roof, where they found a man in the act of dropping a long horsehair line, to which was attached a small hook, through a hole directly over the spot where Laubardemont was sitting. The culprit fled, and that night another failure was recorded against the devil.

But such fiascos availed nothing to save Grandier. Neither did it avail him that, before sentence was finally passed, Sister Claire, broken in body and mind, sobbingly affirmed his innocence, protesting that she did not know what she was saying when she accused him; nor that the mother superior, after two hours of agonizing torture self-imposed, fell on her knees before Laubardemont, made a similar admission, and, passing into the convent orchard, tried to hang herself. The commissioner and his colleagues remained obdurate, averring that these confessions were in themselves evidence of witchcraft, since they could be prompted only by the desire of the devils to save their master from his just fate. In August, 1634, Grandier's doom was pronounced. He was to be put to the torture, strangled, and burned. This judgment was carried out to the letter, save that when the executioner approached to strangle him, the ropes binding him to the stake loosened, and he fell forward among the flames, perishing miserably.

It only remains to analyze this medieval tragedy in the light of modern knowledge. To the people of his own generation Grandier was either a wizard most foul, or the victim of a dastardly plot in which all concerned in harrying him to his death knowingly participated. These opinions posterity long shared. But now it is quite possible to reach another conclusion. That there was a conspiracy is evident even from the facts set down by those hostile to Grandier. On the other hand, it is as unnecessary as it is incredible to believe that the plotters included every one instrumental in fixing on the unhappy curé the crime of witchcraft.

Bearing in mind the discoveries of recent years in the twin fields of physiology and psychology, it seems evident that the conspirators were actually limited in number to Mignon, Barré, Laubardemont, and a few of their intimates. In Laubardemont's case, indeed, there is some reason for supposing that he was more dupe than knave, and is therefore to be placed in the same category as the superstitious monks and townspeople on whom Mignon and Barré so successfully imposed. As to the possessed—the mother superior and her nuns—they may one and all be included in a third group as the unwitting tools of Mignon's vengeance. In fine, it is not only possible but entirely reasonable to regard Mignon as a seventeenth-century forerunner of Mesmer, Elliotson, Esdaile, Braid, Charcot, and the present day exponents of hypnotism; and the nuns as his helpless "subjects," obeying his every command with the fidelity observable to-day in the patients of the Salpêtrière and other centers of hypnotic practice.

The justness of this view is borne out by the facts recorded by contemporary annalists, of which only an outline has been given here. The nuns of Loudun were, as has been said, mostly daughters of the nobility, and were thus, in all likelihood, temperamentally unstable, sensitive, high-strung, nervous. The seclusion of their lives, the monotonous routine of their every-day occupations, and the possibilities afforded for dangerous, morbid introspection, could not but have a baneful effect on such natures, leading inevitably to actual insanity or to hysteria. That the possessed were hysterical is abundantly shown by the descriptions their historians give of the character of their convulsions, contortions, etc., and by the references to the anesthetic, or non-sensitive, spots on their bodies. Now, as we know, the convent at Loudun had been in existence for only a few years before Mignon became its father confessor, and so, we may believe, it fell out that he appeared on the scene precisely when sufficient time had elapsed for environment and heredity to do their deadly work and provoke an epidemic of hysteria.

In those benighted times such attacks were popularly ascribed to possession by evil spirits. The hysterical nuns, as the chronicles tell us, explained their condition to Mignon by informing him that, shortly before the onset of their trouble, they had been haunted by the ghost of their former confessor, Father Moussaut. Here Mignon found his opportunity. Picture him gently rebuking the unhappy women, admonishing them that such a good man as Father Moussaut would never return to torment those who had been in his charge, and insisting that the source of their woes must be sought elsewhere; in, say, some evil disposed person, hostile to Father Moussaut's successor, and hoping, through thus afflicting them, to bring the convent into disrepute and in this way strike a deadly blow at its new father confessor. Who might be this evil disposed person? Who, in truth, save Urbain Grandier?

Picture Mignon, again, observing that his suggestion had taken root in the minds of two of the most emotional and impressionable, the mother superior and Sister Claire. Then would follow a course of lessons designed to aid the suggestion to blossom into open accusation. And presently Mignon would make the discovery that the mother superior and Sister Claire would, when in a hysterical state, blindly obey any command he might make, cease from their convulsions, respond intelligently and at his will to questions put to them, renew their convulsions, lapse even into seeming dementia.

Doubtless he did not grasp the full significance and possibilities of his discovery—had he done so the devils would not have bungled matters so often, and no embarrassing confessions would have been forthcoming. But he saw clearly enough that he had in his hand a mighty weapon against his rival, and history has recorded the manner and effectiveness with which he used it.

II

THE DRUMMER OF TEDWORTH

There have been drummers a plenty in all countries and all ages, but there surely has never been the equal of the drummer of Tedworth. His was the distinction to inspire terror the length and breadth of a kingdom, to set a nation by the ears—nay, even to disturb the peace of Church and Crown.

When the Cromwellian wars broke out, he was in his prime, a stout, sturdy Englishman, suffering, as did his fellows, from the misrule of the Stuarts, and ready for any desperate step that might better his fortunes. Volunteering, therefore, under the man of blood and iron, tradition has it that from the first battle to the last his drum was heard inspiring the revolutionists to mighty deeds of valor. The conflict at an end, Charles beheaded, and the Fifth Monarchy men creating chaos in their noisy efforts to establish the Kingdom of God on earth, he lapsed into an obscurity that endured until the Restoration. Then he reëmerged, not as a veteran living at ease on laurels well won, but as a wandering beggar, roving from shire to shire in quest of alms, which he implored to the accompaniment of fearsome music from his beloved drum.

Thus he journeyed, undisturbed and gaining a sufficient living, until he chanced in the spring of 1661 to invade the quiet Wiltshire village of Tedworth. At that time the interests of Tedworth were identical with the interests of a certain Squire Mompesson, and he, being a gouty, irritable individual, was little disposed to have his peace and the peace of Tedworth disturbed by the drummer's loud bawling and louder drumming. At his orders rough hands seized the unhappy wanderer, blows rained upon him, and he was driven from Tedworth minus his drum. In vain he begged the wrathful Mompesson to restore it to him; in vain, with the tears streaming down his battle-worn, weather-beaten face, he protested that the drum was the only friend left to him in all the world; and in vain he related the happy memories it held for him. "Go," he was roughly told—"go, and be thankful thou escapest so lightly!" So go he did, and whither he went nobody knew, and for the moment nobody cared.

But all Tedworth soon had occasion to wish that his lamentations had moved the Squire to pity. Hardly a month later, when Mompesson had journeyed to the capital to pay his respects to the King, his family were aroused in the middle of the night by angry voices and an incessant banging on the front door. Windows were tried; entrance was vehemently demanded. Within, panic reigned at once. The house was situated in a lonely spot, and it seemed certain that, having heard of its master's absence, a band of highwaymen, with whom the countryside abounded, had planned to turn burglars. The occupants, consisting as they did of women and children, could at best make scant resistance; and consequently there was much quaking and trembling, until, finding the bolts and bars too strong for them, the unwelcome visitors withdrew.

Unmeasured was Mompesson's wrath when he returned and learned of the alarm. He only hoped, he declared, that the villains would venture back—he would give them a greeting such as had not been known since the days of the great war. That very night he had opportunity to make good his boast, for soon after the household had sought repose the disturbance broke out anew. Lighting a lantern, slipping into a dressing-gown, and snatching up a brace of pistols, the Squire dashed down-stairs, the noise becoming louder the nearer he reached the door. Click, clash—the bolts were slipped back, the key was turned, and, lantern extended, he peered into the night.

The moment he opened the door all became still, and nothing but empty darkness met his eyes. Almost immediately, however, the knocking began at a second door, to which, after making the first fast, he hurried, only to find the same result, and to hear, with mounting anger, a tumult at yet another door. Again silence when this was thrown open. But, stepping outside, as he afterward told the story, Mompesson became aware of "a strange and hollow sound in the air." Forthwith the suspicion entered his mind that the noises he had heard might be of supernatural origin. To him, true son of the seventeenth century, a suspicion of this sort was tantamount to certainty, and an unreasoning alarm filled his soul; an alarm that grew into deadly fear when, safe in the bed he had hurriedly sought, a tremendous booming sound came from the top of the house.

Here, in an upper room, for safe-keeping and as an interesting relic of the Civil War, had been placed the beggar's drum, and the terrible thought occurred to Mompesson: "Can it be that the drummer is dead, and that his spirit has returned to torment me?"

A few nights later no room for doubt seemed left. Instead of the nocturnal shouting and knocking, there began a veritable concert from the room containing the drum. This concert, Mompesson informed his friends, opened with a peculiar "hurling in the air over the house," and closed with "the beating of a drum like that at the breaking up of a guard." The mental torture of the Squire and his family may be easier imagined than described. And before long matters grew much worse, when, becoming emboldened, the ghostly drummer laid aside his drum to play practical, and sometimes exceedingly painful, jokes on the members of the household.

Curiously enough, his malice was chiefly directed against Mompesson's children, who—poor little dears—had certainly never worked him any injury. Yet we are told that for a time "it haunted none particularly but them." When they were in bed the coverings were dragged off and thrown on the floor; there was heard a scratching noise under the bed as of some animal with iron claws; sometimes they were lifted bodily, "so that six men could not hold them down," and their limbs were beaten violently against the bedposts. Nor did the unseen and unruly visitant scruple to plague Mompesson's aged mother, whose Bible was frequently hidden from her, and in whose bed ashes, knives, and other articles were placed.

As time passed marvels multiplied. The assurance is solemnly given that "chairs moved of themselves." A board, it is insisted, rose out of the floor of its own accord and flung itself violently at a servant. Strange lights, "like corpse candles," floated about. The Squire's personal attendant John, "a stout fellow and of sober conversation," was one night confronted by a ghastly apparition in the form of "a great body with two red and glaring eyes." Frequently, too, when John was in bed he was treated as were the children, his coverings removed, his body struck, etc. But it was noticed that whenever he grasped and brandished a sword he was left in peace. Clearly, the ghost had a healthy respect for cold steel.

It had less respect for exorcising, which, of course, was tried, but tried in vain. All went well as long as the clergyman was on his knees saying the prescribed prayers by the bedside of the tormented children, but the moment he rose a bed staff was thrown at him and other articles of furniture danced about so madly that body and limb were endangered.

Mompesson was at his wits' end. Well might he be! Apart from the injury done to his family and belongings, his house was thronged night and day by inquisitive visitors from all sections of the country. He was denounced on the one hand as a trickster, and on the other as a man who must be guilty of some terrible secret sin, else he would not thus be vexed. Sermons were preached with him as the text. Factions were formed, angrily affirming and denying the supernatural character of the disturbances. News of the affair traveled even to the ears of the King, who dispatched an investigating commission to Mompesson House, where, greatly to the delight of the unbelieving, nothing untoward occurred during the commissioners' visit. But thereafter, as if to make up for lost time, the most sensational and vexatious phenomena of the haunting were produced.

Thus matters continued for many months, until it dawned on Mompesson and his friends that possibly the case was not one of ghosts but one of witchcraft. This suspicion rose from the singular circumstance that voices in the children's room began, "for a hundred times together," to cry "A witch! A witch!" Resolved to put matters to a test, one of the boldest of a company of spectators suddenly demanded, "Satan, if the drummer set thee to work, give three knocks and no more!" To which three knocks were distinctly heard, and afterward, by way of confirmation, five knocks as requested by another onlooker.

Now began an eager hunt for the once despised drummer, who was presently found in jail at Gloucester accused of theft. And with this discovery word was brought to Mompesson that the drummer had openly boasted of having bewitched him. This was enough for the outraged Squire. There was in existence an act of King James I. holding it a felony to "feed, employ, or reward any evil spirit," and under its provisions he speedily had his alleged persecutor indicted as a wizard.

Amid great excitement the aged veteran was brought from Gloucester to Salisbury to stand trial. But his spirit remained unbroken. Instead of confessing, humbly begging mercy, and promising amends, he undertook to bargain with

Mompesson, promising that if the latter secured his liberty and gave him employment as a farm hand, he would rid him of the haunting. Perhaps because he feared treachery, perhaps because, as he said, he felt sure the drummer "could do him no good in any honest way," Mompesson rejected this ingenuous proposal.

So the drummer was left to his fate, which, for those days, was most unexpected. A packed and attentive court room listened to the tale of the mishaps and misadventures that had made Mompesson House a national center of interest; it was proved that the accused had been intimate with an old vagabond who pretended to possess supernatural powers; and emphasis was laid on the alleged fact that he had boasted of having revenged himself on Mompesson for the confiscation of his drum. Luckily for him, Mompesson was not the power in Salisbury that he was in Tedworth, and the drummer's eloquent defense moved the jury to acquit him and to send him on his way rejoicing. Thereafter he was never again heard of in Wiltshire or in the pages of history, and with his disappearance came an end to the knockings, the corpse candles, and all the other uncanny phenomena that had made life a ceaseless nightmare for the Mompessons.

Such is the astonishing story of the drummer of Tedworth, still cited by the superstitious as a capital example of the intermeddling of superhuman agencies in human affairs, and still mentioned by the skeptical as one of the most amusing and most successful hoaxes on record.

To us of the twentieth century its chief significance lies in the striking resemblance between the tribulations of the Mompesson family and the so-called physical phenomena of modern spiritism. All who have attended spiritistic séances are familiar with the invisible and perverse ghost, which, for no apparent reason other than to mystify, causes furniture to gyrate violently, rings bells, plays tambourines, levitates the "medium," and favors the spectators with sundry taps, pinches, even blows. Precisely thus was it with the doings at Mompesson House, where many of the salient phenomena of modern spiritism were anticipated nearly two hundred and fifty years ago.

The inference is irresistible that a more or less intimate connection exists between the disturbances at Tedworth and the triumphs of latter-day mediumship, and it thus becomes doubly interesting to examine the evidence for and against the supernatural origin of the performances that so perplexed the Englishmen of the Restoration. This evidence is presented in far greater detail than is here possible, in a curious document written by the Reverend Joseph Glanvill, a clergyman of the Church of England and an eye witness of some of the phenomena. His point of view is that of an ardent believer in the verity of witchcraft, and his narrative of the Tedworth affair finds place in a treatise designed to discomfit those irreligious persons who maintained the opposite. It is therefore evident that his account of the case is to be regarded as a piece of special pleading, and as such must be received with critical caution.

The need for caution is further emphasized by the important circumstance that of all the phenomena described, only those most susceptible of mundane interpretation were witnessed by Glanvill or Mompesson. All of the more extraordinary—the great body with the red and glaring eyes, the levitated children, etc.—came to the narrator from second or third or fourth hand sources not always clearly indicated, and doubtless uneducated and superstitious persons, such as peasants or servants, whose fears would lend wings to their imagination.

Keeping these facts before us, what do we find? We find that, so far from supporting the supernatural view, the evidence points to a systematic course of fraud and deceit carried out, not by the drummer, not by Mompesson and Glanvill (as many of that generation were unkind enough to suggest), not by the Mompesson servants, but by the Mompesson children, and particularly by the oldest child, a girl of ten.

It was about the children that the disturbances centered, it was in their room that the manifestations usually took place, and—what should have served to direct suspicion to them at once—when, in the hope of affording them relief, their father separated them, sending the youngest to lodge with a neighbor and taking the oldest into his own room, it was remarked that the neighbor's house immediately became the scene of demoniac activity, as did the Squire's apartment, which had previously been virtually undisturbed. Here and now developed a phenomenon that places little Miss Mompesson on a par with the celebrated Fox sisters, for her father's bed chamber was turned into a séance room in which messages were rapped out very much as messages have been rapped out ever since the fateful night in 1848 that saw modern spiritism ushered into the world.

Glanvill's personal testimony, the most precise and circumstantial in the entire case, strongly, albeit unwittingly, supports this view of the affair. It appears that he passed only one night in the haunted house, and of his several experiences there is none that cannot be set down to fraud plus imagination, with the children the active agents. Witness the following from his story of what he heard and beheld in the oft-mentioned "children's room":

"At this time it used to haunt the children, and that as soon as they were laid. They went to bed the night I was there about eight of the clock, when a maid servant, coming down from them, told us that it was come.... Mr. Mompesson and I and a gentleman that came with me went up. I heard a strange scratching as I went up the stairs, and when we came into the room I perceived *it was just behind the bolster of the children's bed and seemed to be against the tick. It was as loud a scratching as one with long nails could make upon a bolster.* There were two modest little girls in the bed, between seven and eight years old, as I guessed. I saw their hands out of the clothes, and they could not contribute to the noise that was behind their heads. *They had been used to it and still had somebody or other in the chamber with them, and therefore seemed not to be much affrighted.*

"I, standing at the bed's head, thrust my hand behind the bolster, directing it to the place whence the noise seemed to come. *Whereupon the noise ceased there, and was heard in another part of the bed; but when I had taken out my hand it returned and was heard in the same place as before.* I had been told it would imitate noises, and made trial by scratching several times upon the sheet, as five, and seven, and ten, which it followed, and still stopped at my number. I searched under and behind the bed, turned up the clothes to the bed cords, grasped the bolster, sounded the wall behind, and made all the search that possibly I could, to find if there were any trick, contrivance, or common cause of it. The like did my friend, but we could discover nothing.

"So that I was then verily persuaded, and am so still, that the noise was made by some demon or spirit."

Doubtless his countenance betrayed the receptiveness of his mind, and it is not surprising that the naughty little girls proceeded to work industriously upon his imagination. He speaks of having heard under the bed a panting sound, which, he is certain, caused "a motion so strong that it shook the room and windows very sensibly"; and it also appears that he was induced to believe that he saw something moving in a "linen bag" hanging in the room, which bag, on being emptied, was found to contain nothing animate. Therefore—spirits again! After bidding the children good night and retiring to the room set apart for him, he was wakened from a sound sleep by a tremendous knocking on his door, and to his terrified inquiry, "In the name of God, who is it, and what would you have?" received the not wholly reassuring reply, "Nothing with you." In the morning, when he spoke of the incident and remarked that he supposed a servant must have rapped at the wrong door, he learned to his profound astonishment that "no one of the house lay that way or had business thereabout." This being so, it could not possibly have been anything but a ghost.

Thus runs the argument of the superstitious clergyman. And all the while, we may feel tolerably sure, little Miss Mompesson was chuckling inwardly at the panic into which she had thrown the reverend gentleman.

If it be objected that no girl of ten could successfully execute such a sustained imposture, one need only point to the many instances in which children of equally tender years or little older have since ventured on similar mystifications, with even more startling results. Incredible as it may seem to those who have not looked into the subject, it is a fact that there are boys and girls—especially girls—who take a morbid delight in playing pranks that will astound and perplex their elders. The mere suggestion that Satan or a discarnate spirit is at the bottom of the mischief will then act as a powerful stimulus to the elaboration of even more sensational performances, and the result, if detection does not soon occur, will be a full-fledged "poltergeist," as the crockery-breaking, furniture-throwing ghost is technically called.

The singular affair of Hetty Wesley, which we shall take up next, is a case in point. So, too, is the history of the Fox sisters, who were extremely juvenile when they discovered the possibilities latent in the properly manipulated rap and knock. And the spirits who so maliciously disturbed the peace of good old Dr. Phelps in Stratford, Connecticut, a half century and more ago, unquestionably owed their being to the nimble wit and abnormal fancy of his two step-children, aged sixteen and eleven.

It is to be remembered, further, that contemporary conditions were exceptionally favorable to the success of the Tedworth hoax. In all likelihood the children had nothing to do with the first alarm, the alarm that occurred during Mompesson's absence in London; and possibly the second was only a rude practical joke by some village lads who had heard of the first and wished to put the Squire's courage to a test. But once the little Mompessons learned, or suspected, that their father associated the noises with the vagrant drummer, a wide vista of enjoyment would open before their mischief-loving minds. Entering on a career of mystification, they would find the road made easy by the gullibility of those about them; and the chances are that had they been caught *in flagrante delicto* they would have put in the plea that fraudulent mediums so frequently offer to-day—"An evil spirit took possession of me." As it was, the superstition of the times—and doubtless the rats and shaky timbers of Mompesson House did their part—was their constant and unfailing support. Everything that happened would be magnified and distorted by the witnesses, either at the moment or in retrospect, until in the end the Rev. Mr. Glanvill, recording honestly enough what he himself had seen, could find material for a history of the most marvelous marvels.

In short, the more closely one examines the details of the Tedworth mystery, the more will he find himself in agreement with George Cruikshank's brutally frank opinion:

"All this seems very strange, about this drummer and his drum; But for myself I really think this drumming ghost was all a hum."

III

THE HAUNTING OF THE WESLEYS

The Rev. Samuel Wesley is chiefly known to posterity as the father of the famous John Wesley, the founder of Methodism, and of the hardly less famous Charles Wesley. But the Rev. Samuel has further claims to remembrance. If he gave to the world John and Charles Wesley, he was also the sire of seventeen other Wesleys, eight of whom, like their celebrated brothers, grew to maturity and attained varying degrees of distinction.

He was himself a man of distinction as preacher, poet, and controversialist. His sermons were sermons in the good, old-fashioned sense of the term. His poems were the despair of the critics, but won him a wide reputation. He was an adept in what Whistler called the gentle art of making enemies. Though more familiar with the inside of a pulpit, he was not unacquainted with the inside of a jail. He raised his numerous progeny on an income seldom exceeding one thousand dollars a year. And, what is perhaps the most astonishing fact in a career replete with surprises, he was the hero of one of the best authenticated ghost stories on record.

This visitation from the supermundane came as a climax to a series of worldly annoyances that would have upset the equanimity of a very Job—and the Rev. Samuel, in temper at any rate, was the reverse of Job-like. His troubles began in the closing years of the seventeenth century, when he became rector of the established church at Epworth, Lincolnshire, a venerable edifice dating back to the stormy days of Edward II., and as damp as it was old. The story goes that this living was granted him as a reward because he dedicated one of his poems to Queen Mary. But the Queen would seem to have had punishment in mind for him, rather than reward.

Located in the Isle of Axholme, in the midst of a long stretch of fen country bounded by four rivers, and for a great part under water, Epworth was at that epoch dreariness itself. The Rev. Samuel's spirits must have sunk within him as the carts bearing his already large family and his few household belongings toiled through quagmire and morass; they must have fallen still farther when he gazed down the one straggling street at the rectory of mud and thatch that was to be his home; and they must have touched the zero mark, zealous High Churchman that he was, with the discovery that his peasant parishioners were Presbyterian-minded folk who hated ritualism as cordially as they hated the Pope.

Whatever his secret sentiments, he lost no time in endeavoring to stamp the imprint of his vigorous personality on Epworth. Forgetful, or unheedful, of the fact that the natives of the Isle of Axholme were notoriously violent and lawless, he began to rule them with a rod of iron. Thus they should think, thus they should do, thus they should go! Above all, the Rev. Samuel never permitted them to forget that in addition to spiritual they owed him temporal obligations. In the matter of tithes—always a sore subject in a community hard put to extract a living from the soil—he was unrelenting.

Necessity may have driven him; but it was only to be expected that murmurings should arise, and from words the angry islanders passed to deeds. For a time they contented themselves with burning the rector's barn and trying to burn his house. Then, when he was so indiscreet as to become indebted to one of their number, they clapped him into prison. His speedy release, through the intervention of clerical friends, and his blunt refusal to seek a new sphere of activity, were followed by more barn burning, by the slaughter of his cattle, and finally by a fire that utterly destroyed the rectory and all but cost the lives of several of its inmates, who by that time included the future father of Methodism.

The bravery with which the Rev. Samuel met this crowning disaster, and the energy with which he set about the task of rebuilding his home—not in mud and thatch, but in substantial brick—seem to have shamed the villagers into giving him peace, seem even to have inspired them with a genuine regard for him. He for his part, if we read the difficult pages of his biographers aright, appears to have grown less exacting and more diplomatic. In any event, he was left in quiet to prepare his sermons, write his poems, and assist his devoted wife (who, by the way, he is said to have deserted for an entire year because of a little difference of opinion respecting the right of William of Orange to the English crown) in the upbringing of their children. Thus his life ran along in comparative smoothness until the momentous advent of the ghost.

This unexpected and unwelcome visitor made its first appearance early in December, 1716. At the time the Wesley boys were away from home, but the household was still sufficiently numerous, consisting of the Rev. Samuel, Mrs. Wesley, seven daughters,—Emilia, Susannah, Maria, Mehetabel, Anne, Martha, and Kezziah,—a man servant named Robert Brown, and a maid servant known as Nanny Marshall. Nanny was the first to whom the ghost paid its respects, in a series of blood-curdling groans that "caused the upstarting of her hair, and made her ears prick forth at an unusual rate." In modern parlance, she was greatly alarmed, and hastened to tell the Misses Wesley of the extraordinary noises, which, she assured them, sounded exactly like the groans of a dying man. The derisive laughter of the young women left her state of mind unchanged; and they too gave way to alarm when, a night or so later, loud knocks began to be heard in different parts of the house, accompanied by sundry "groans, squeaks, and tinglings."

Oddly enough, the only member of the family unvisited by the ghost was the Rev. Samuel, and upon learning that he had heard none of the direful sounds his wife and children made up their minds that his death was imminent; for a local superstition had it that in all such cases of haunting the person undisturbed is marked for an early demise. But the worthy clergyman continued hale and hearty, as did the ghost, whose knockings, indeed, soon grew so terrifying that "few or none of the family durst be alone." It was then resolved that, whatever the noises portended, counsel and aid must be sought from the head of the household. At first the Rev. Samuel listened in silence to his spouse's recital; but as she proceeded he burst into a storm of wrath. A ghost? Stuff and nonsense! Not a bit of it! Only some mischief-makers bent on plaguing them. Possibly, and his choler rose higher, a trick played by his daughters themselves, or by their lovers.

Now it was the turn of the Wesley girls to become angry, and we read that they forthwith showed themselves exceedingly "desirous of its continuance till he was convinced." Their desire was speedily granted. The very next night paterfamilias had no sooner tumbled into bed than there came nine resounding knocks "just by his bedside." In an instant he was up and groping for a light. "You heard it, then?" we may imagine Mrs. Wesley anxiously asking, and we may also imagine the robust Anglo-Saxon of his response.

Another night and more knockings, followed by "a noise in the room over our heads, as if several people were walking." This time, to quote further from Mrs. Wesley's narrative as given in a letter to her absent son Samuel, the tumult "was so outrageous that we thought the children would be frightened; so your father and I rose, and went down in the dark to light a candle. Just as we came to the bottom of the broad stairs, having hold of each other, on my side there seemed as if somebody had emptied a bag of money at my feet; and on his, as if all the bottles under the stairs (which were many) had been dashed in a thousand pieces. We passed through the hall into the kitchen, and got a candle and went to see the children, whom we found asleep."

With this the Rev. Samuel seems to have come round to the family's way of thinking; for in the morning he sent a messenger to the nearby village of Haxey with the request that the vicar of Haxey, a certain Mr. Hoole, would ride over and assist him in "conjuring" the evil spirit out of his house. Burning with curiosity, Mr. Hoole made such good time to Epworth that before noon he was at the rectory and eagerly listening to an account of the marvels that had so alarmed the Wesleys.

In addition to the phenomena already set forth, he learned that while the knocks were heard in all parts of the house, they were most frequent in the children's room; that at prayers they almost invariably interrupted the family's devotions, especially when Mr. Wesley began the prayers for King George and the Prince of Wales, from which it was inferred that the ghost was a Jacobite; that often a sound was heard like the rocking of a cradle, and another sound like the gobbling of a turkey, and yet another "something like a man, in a loose nightgown trailing after him"; and that if one stamped his foot, "Old Jeffrey," as the younger children had named the ghost, would knock precisely as many times as there had been stampings.

None of these major marvels was vouchsafed to Mr. Hoole; but he heard knockings in plenty, and, after a night of terror, made haste back to Haxey, having lost all desire to play the rôle of exorcist. His fears may possibly have been increased by the violence of Mr. Wesley, who, after vainly exhorting the ghost to speak out and tell his business, flourished a pistol and threatened to discharge it in the direction whence the knockings came. This was too much for peace-loving, spook-fearing Mr. Hoole. "Sir," he protested, "you are convinced this is something preternatural. If so, you cannot hurt it; but you give it power to hurt you." The logic of Mr. Hoole's argument is hardly so evident as his panic. Off he galloped, leaving the Rev. Samuel to lay the ghost as best he could.

After his departure wonders grew apace. Thus far the manifestations had been wholly auditory; now visual phenomena were added. One evening Mrs. Wesley beheld something dart out from beneath a bed and quickly disappear. Sister Emilia, who was present, reported to brother Samuel that this something was "like a badger, only without any head that was discernible." The same apparition came to confound the man servant, Robert Brown, once in the badger form, and once in the form of a white rabbit which "turned round before him several times." Robert was also the witness of an even more peculiar performance by the elusive ghost. "Being grinding corn in the garrets, and happening to stop a little, the handle of the mill was turn [sic] round with great swiftness." It is interesting to note that Robert subsequently declared that "nothing vexed him but that the mill was empty. If corn had been in it, Old Jeffrey might have ground his heart out for him; he would never have disturbed him." More annoying was a habit into which the ghost fell of rattling latches, jingling warming pans and other metal utensils, and brushing rudely against people in the dark. "Thrice," asserted the Rev. Samuel, "I have been pushed by an invisible power, once against the corner of my desk in the study, a second time against the door of the matted chamber, a third time against the right side of the frame of my study door."

On at least one occasion Old Jeffrey indulged in a pastime popular with the spiritistic mediums of a later day. John Wesley tells us, on the authority of sister Nancy, that one night, when she was playing cards with some of the many other sisters, the bed on which she sat was suddenly lifted from the ground. "She leapt down and said, 'Surely Old Jeffrey would not run away with her.' However, they persuaded her to sit down again, which she had scarce done when it was again lifted up several times successively, a considerable height, upon which she left her seat and would not be prevailed upon to sit there any more."

Clearly, the Wesley family were in a bad way. Entreaties, threats, exorcism, had alike failed to banish the obstinate ghost. But though they knew it not, relief was at hand. Whether repenting of his misdoings, or desirous of seeking pastures new, Jeffrey, after a visitation lasting nearly two months, took his departure almost as unceremoniously as he had arrived, and left the unhappy Wesleys to resume by slow degrees their wonted ways of life.

Such is the story unfolded by the Wesleys themselves in a series of letters and memoranda, which, taken together, form, as was said, one of the best authenticated narratives of haunting extant. But before endeavoring to ascertain the source of the phenomena credited to the soi-disant Jeffrey, another and fully as important inquiry must be made. What, it is necessary to ask, did the Wesleys actually hear and see in the course of the two months that they had their ghost with them? The answer obviously must be sought through an analysis of the evidence for the haunting. This chronologically falls into three divisions. The first consists of letters addressed to young Samuel Wesley by his father, mother, and two of his sisters, and written at the time of the disturbances; the second, of letters written by Mrs. Wesley and four of her daughters to John Wesley in the summer and autumn of 1726 (that is to say, more than nine years after the haunting), of an account written by the senior Samuel Wesley, and of statements by Hoole and Robert Brown; the third, of an article contributed to "The Arminian Magazine" in 1784 (nearly seventy years after the event) by John Wesley.

Now, the most cursory examination of the various documents shows remarkable discrepancies between the earlier and later versions. Writing to her son Samuel, when the ghost was still active, and she would not be likely to minimize its doings, Mrs. Wesley thus describes the first occurrences:

"On the first of December, our maid heard, at the door of the dining-room, several dismal groans like a person in extremes, at the point of death. We gave little heed to her relation and endeavored to laugh her out of her fears. Some nights (two or three) after, several of the family heard a strange knocking in divers places, usually three or four knocks at a time, and then stayed a little. This continued every night for a fortnight; sometimes it was in the garret, but most commonly in the nursery, or green chamber."

Contrast with this the portion of John Wesley's "Arminian Magazine" article referring to the same period:

"On the second of December, 1716, while Robert Brown, my father's servant, was sitting with one of the maids, a little before ten at night, in the dining-room which opened into the garden, they both heard one knocking at the door. Robert rose and opened it, but could see nobody. Quickly it knocked again and groaned.... He opened the door again twice or thrice, the knocking being twice or thrice repeated; but still seeing nothing, and being a little startled, they rose and went up to bed. When Robert came to the top of the garret stairs, he saw a handmill, which was at a little distance, whirled about very swiftly.... When he was in bed, he heard as it were the gobbling of a turkey cock close to the bedside; and soon after, the sound of one stumbling over his shoes and boots; but there were none there, he had left them below.... The next evening, between five and six o'clock, my sister Molly, then about twenty years of age, sitting in the dining-room reading, heard as if it were the door that led into the hall open, and a person walking in, that seemed to have on a silk nightgown, rustling and trailing along. It seemed to walk round her, then to the door, then round again; but she could see nothing."

As a matter of fact, the contemporary records are silent respecting the extraordinary happenings that overshadow all else in the records of 1726 and 1784. In the former, for example, we find no reference to the affair of the mill handle, the levitation of the bed, the rude bumpings given to Mr. Wesley. There is much talk of knockings and groanings, of sounds like footsteps, rustling silks, falling coals, breaking bottles, and moving latches; allusion is made to the badger like and rabbit like apparition; and there is mention of a peculiar dancing of father's "trencher" without "anybody's stirring the table"; but the sum total makes very tame reading compared with the material to be found in the accounts written in after years and commonly utilized—as it has been utilized here—to form the narrative of the haunting. Not only this, but a rigorous division of the contemporary evidence into first hand and second hand still further eliminates the element of the marvelous. Admitting as evidence only the fact set forth as having been observed by the relators themselves, the haunting is reduced to a matter of knocks, groans, tinglings, squeaks, creakings, crashings, and footsteps.

We are, therefore, justified in believing that in this case, like so many others of its kind, the fallibility of human memory has played an overwhelming part in exaggerating the experiences actually undergone; that, in fine, nothing occurred in the rectory at Epworth, between December 1, 1716, and January 31, 1717, that may not be attributed to human agency.

Who, then, was the agent? Knowing what we do of Wesley's previous relations with the villagers, the first impulse is to place the responsibility at their door. But for this there is no real warrant. Years had elapsed since the culminating catastrophe of the burning of the rectory, and in the interim matters had been put on an amicable basis. Moreover, the evidence as to the haunting itself goes to show that the phenomena could not possibly have been produced by a person, or persons, operating from outdoors; but must, on the contrary, have been the work of some one intimately acquainted with the arrangements of the house and enjoying the full confidence of its master.

Thus our inquiry narrows to the inmates of the rectory. Of these, Mr. and Mrs. Wesley, may at once be left out of consideration, as also may the servants, all accounts agreeing that from the outset they were genuinely alarmed. There remain only the Wesley girls, and our effort must be to discover which of them was the culprit.

At first blush this seems an impossible task; but let us scan the evidence carefully. We find, to begin with, that only four of the seven sisters are represented in the correspondence relating to the haunting. Two of the others, Kezziah and Martha, were mere children and not of letter-writing age, and their silence in the matter is thus satisfactorily accounted for. But that the third, Mehetabel, should likewise be silent is distinctly puzzling. Not only was she quite able to give an account of her experiences (she was at least between eighteen and nineteen years of age), but it is known that she had a veritable passion for pen and ink, a passion which in after years won her no mean reputation as a poetess. And, more than this, she seems to have enjoyed a far greater share of Jeffrey's attentions than did any other member of the family. "My sister Hetty, I find," remarks the observing Samuel, "was more particularly troubled." And Emilia declares, almost in the language of complaint, that "it was never near me, except two or three times, and never followed me as it did my sister Hetty."

Manifestly, it may be worth while to inquire into the history and characteristics of this young woman. Her biographer, Dr. Adam Clarke, informs us that "from her childhood she was gay and sprightly; full of mirth, good humor, and keen wit. She indulged this disposition so much that it was said to have given great uneasiness to her parents; because she was in consequence often betrayed into inadvertencies which, though of small moment in themselves, showed that her mind was not under proper discipline; and that fancy, not reason, often dictated that line of conduct which she thought proper to pursue."

This information is the more interesting, in the present connection, since it contrasts strongly with the unqualified commendation Dr. Clarke accords the other sisters. From the same authority we learn that as a child Miss Mehetabel was so precocious that at the age of eight she could read the Greek Testament in the original; that she was from her earliest youth emotional and sentimental; that despite her intellectual tastes and attainments she gave her hand to an illiterate journeyman plumber and glazier; and that when the fruit of this union lay dying by her side she insisted on dictating to her husband a poem afterward published under the moving caption of "A Mother's Address to Her Dying Infant." Another of her poems, by the way, is significantly entitled, "The Lucid Interval."

There can, then, be little question that Hetty Wesley was precisely the type of girl to derive amusement by working on the superstitious fears of those about her. We find, too, in the evidence itself certain fugitive references directly pointing to her as the creator of Old Jeffrey. It seems that she had a practice of sitting up and moving about the house long after all the other inmates, except her father, had retired for the night. The ghost was especially noisy and malevolent when in her vicinity, knocking boisterously on the bed in which she slept, and even knocking under her feet. And what is most suggestive, two witnesses, her father and her sister Susannah, testify that on some occasions the noises failed to wake her, but caused her "to tremble exceedingly in her sleep." It must, indeed, have been a difficult matter to restrain laughter at the spectacle of the night-gowned, night-capped, much bewildered parson, candle in one hand and pistol in the other, peering under and about the bed in quest of the invisible ghost.

To be sure, it is impossible to adduce positive proof that Hetty Wesley and Old Jeffrey were one and the same. But the evidence supports this view of the case as it supports no other, and, taken in conjunction with the facts of her earlier and later life, leaves little doubt that had the Rev. Samuel paid closer attention to the comings and goings of this particular daughter the ghost that so sorely tried him would have taken its flight much sooner than it did. Her motive for the deception must be left to conjecture. In all probability it was only the desire to amaze and terrorize, a desire as was said before, not infrequently operative along similar lines in the case of young people of a lively disposition and morbid imagination.

IV

THE VISIONS OF EMANUEL SWEDENBORG

In mid April of the memorable year 1745, two men, hastening through a busy London thoroughfare, paused for a moment to follow with their eyes a third, whom they had greeted but who had passed without so much as a glance in their direction. The face of one betrayed chagrin; but the other smiled amusedly.

"You must not mind, dear fellow," said he; "that is only Swedenborg's way, as you will discover when you know him better. His feet are on the earth; but for the moment his mind is in the clouds, pondering some solution to the wonderful problems he has set himself, marvelous man that he is."

"Yet," objected the other, "he seems such a thorough man of the world, so finely dressed, so courtly as a rule in speech and manner."

"He is a man of the world, a true cosmopolitan," was the quick response. "I warrant few are so widely and so favorably known. He is as much at home in London, Paris, Berlin, Dresden, Amsterdam, or Copenhagen as in his native city of Stockholm. Kings and Queens, grand dames and gallant wits, statesmen and soldiers, scientists and philosophers, find pleasure in his society. He can meet all on their own ground, and to all he has something fresh and interesting to say. But he is nevertheless, and above everything else, a dreamer."

"A dreamer?"

"Aye. They tell me that he will not rest content until he has found the seat of the soul in man. Up through mathematics, mechanics, mineralogy, astronomy, chemistry, even physiology, has he gone, mastering every science in turn, until he is now perhaps the most learned man in Europe. But his learning satisfies him not a whit, since the soul still eludes him,—and eludes him, mark you, despite month upon month of toil in the dissecting room. If the study of anatomy fail him, I know not where he will next turn. For my part, I fancy he need not look beyond the stomach. The wonder is that his own stomach has not given him the clue ere this; for, metaphysician though he be, he enjoys the good things of earth. Let me tell you a story—"

Thus, chatting and laughing, the friends continued on their way, every step taking them farther from the unwitting subject of their words. He, for his part, absorbed in thought, pressed steadily forward to his destination, a quiet inn in a sequestered quarter of the city. The familiar sounds of eighteenth-century London—the bawling of apprentices shouting their masters' wares, the crying of fishwives, the quarreling of drunkards, the barking of curs, the bellowing of cattle on their way to market and slaughter house—broke unheeded about him.

He was, as the gossip had put it, in the clouds, intent on the riddles his learning had rendered only the more complex, riddles having to do with the nature of the universe and with man's place in the universe. Nor did he rouse himself from his meditations until the door of the inn had closed behind him and he found himself in its common room. Then he became the Emanuel

Swedenborg of benignity, geniality, and courtesy, the Swedenborg whom all men loved.

"I am going to my room," said he to the innkeeper, in charming, broken English, "and I wish to be served there. I find I am very hungry; so see that you spare not."

While he is standing at the window, waiting for his dinner, and gazing abstractedly into the ill-paved, muddy street illumined by a transitory gleam of April sunshine, let us try to gain a closer view of him than that afforded by the brief account of his unrecognized acquaintance. The attempt will be worth while; for at this very moment he has, all unconsciously, reached the great crisis of his life, and is about to leave behind him the achievements of his earlier years, setting himself instead to tasks of a very different nature. We see him, then, a man nearing the age of sixty, of rather more than average height, smooth shaven, bewigged, bespectacled, and scrupulously dressed according to the fashion of the day. Time in its passing has dealt gently with him. There is no stoop to his shoulders, no tremor in the fingers that play restlessly on the window-pane. Not a wrinkle mars the placid features.

Well may he feel at peace with the world. His whole career has been a steady progress, his record that of one who has attempted many things and failed in few. Before he was twenty-one his learning had gained for him a doctorate in philosophy. Then, enthusiastic, open-minded, and open-eyed, he had hurried abroad, to pursue in England, Holland, France, and Germany his chosen studies of mathematics, mechanics, and astronomy. Returning to Sweden to assume the duties of assessor of mines, he speedily proved that he was no mere theorizer, his inventive genius enabling the warlike Charles XII. to transport overland galleys and sloops for the siege of Frederikshald, sea passage being barred by hostile fleets. Ennobled for this feat, he plunged with ardor into the complicated problems of statecraft, problems rendered the more difficult by the economic distress in which Charles's wars had involved his Kingdom. Here again he attained distinction.

Yet always the problems of science and philosophy claimed his chief devotion. From the study of stars and minerals he passed to the contemplation of other marvels of nature as revealed in man himself. And now behold him turned chemist, anatomist, physiologist, and psychologist, and repeating in these fields of research his former triumphs. Still, indomitable man, he refused to stop. He would press on, far beyond the confines of what his generation held to be the knowable. "The end of the senses," to quote his own words, "is that God may be seen." He would peer into the innermost recesses of man's being, to discern the soul of man, mayhap to discern God himself.

But, if he were scientist and metaphysician, he was also human, and that pleasant April afternoon the humanity in him bulked large when he finally turned from the window and took his seat at the bountifully heaped table. He was, as he had told the innkeeper, very hungry, and he ate with a zest that abundantly confirmed his statement. How pleasant the odors from this dish and that—how agreeable the flavor of everything! Surely he had never enjoyed meal more, and surely he was no longer "in the clouds"; but was instead recalling pleasant reminiscences of his doings in one and another of the gay capitals of Europe! There would be not a little to bring a twinkle of delight to his beaming eyes, not a little to soften his scholastic lips into a gentle smile. And so, in solitary state, he ate and drank, with nothing to warn him of the impending and momentous change that was to shape anew his career and his view-point.

Conceive his astonishment, therefore, when, his dinner still unfinished, he felt a strange languor creeping over him and a mysterious obscurity dimming his eyes. Conceive, further, his horror at sight of the floor about him covered with frogs and toads and snakes and creeping things. And picture, finally, his amazement when, the darkness that enveloped him suddenly clearing, he beheld a man sitting in the far corner of the room and eying him, as it seemed, reproachfully, even disdainfully.

In vain, he essayed to rise, to lift his hand, to speak. Invisible bonds held him in his chair, an unseen power kept him mute. For an instant he fancied that he must be dreaming; but the noises from outdoors and the sight of the table and food before him brought conviction that he was in full possession of his senses. Now his visitor spoke, and spoke only four words, which astonished no less than alarmed him. "Eat not so much." Only this—then utter silence. Again the enveloping darkness—frogs, toads, snakes, faded in its depths—and with returning light Swedenborg was once more alone in the room.

Small wonder that the remaining hours of the day were spent in fruitless cogitation of this weird and disagreeable experience which far transcended metaphysician's normal ken. Nor is it surprising to find him naïvely admitting that "this unexpected event hastened my return home." Imagination can easily round out the picture,—the rising in terror, the overturning of the chair, the seizing of cocked hat and gold-headed cane, the few explanatory words to the astonished innkeeper, the hurried departure, and the progress, perchance at a more rapid gait than usual, to the sleeping quarters in another section of the town. Arrived there, safe in the refuge of his commodious bed-room, sage argument would follow in the effort to attain persuasion that the terrifying vision had been but "the effect of accidental causes." Be sure, though, that our philosopher, dreading a return of the specter if he permitted food to pass his lips, would go hungry to bed that night.

That night—more visions. To the wakeful, restless, perturbed Swedenborg the same figure appeared, this time without snakes or frogs or toads, and not in darkness, but in the midst of a great white light that filled the bed chamber with a wonderful radiance. Then a voice spoke:

"I am God the Lord, the Creator and Redeemer of the world. I have chosen thee to lay before men the spiritual sense of the Holy Word. I will teach thee what thou art to write."

Slowly the light faded, the figure disappeared. And now the astounded philosopher, his amazement growing with each passing moment, found himself transported as it seemed to another world,—the world of the dead. Men and women of his acquaintance greeted him as they had been wont to do when on earth, pressed about him, eagerly questioned him. Their faces still wore the familiar expressions of kindliness, anxiety, sincerity, ill will, as the case might be. In every way they appeared to be still numbered among the living. They were clad in the clothes they had been accustomed to wear, they ate and drank, they lived in houses and towns. The philosophers among them continued to dispute, the clergy to admonish, the authors to write.

But, his perception enlarging, Swedenborg presently discovered that this was in reality only an intermediate state of existence; that beyond it at the one end was heaven and at the other hell, to one or the other of which the dead ultimately gravitated according to their desires and conduct. For, as he was to learn later, the spiritual world was a world of law and order fully as much as was the natural world. Men were free to do as they chose; but they must bear the consequences. If they were evil-minded, it would be their wish to consort with those of like mind, and in time they must pass to the abode of the wicked; if pure-minded, they would seek out kindred spirits, and, when finally purged of the dross of earth, be translated to the realm of bliss. To heaven, then, voyaged Swedenborg, on a journey of discovery; and to hell likewise. What he saw he has set down in many bulky volumes, than which philosopher has written none more strange.

With the return of daylight it might seem that he would be prompt to dismiss all memory of these peculiar experiences as fantasies of sleep. But he was satisfied that he had not slept; that on the contrary he had been preternaturally conscious throughout the long, eventful night. In solemn retrospect he retraced his past career. He remembered that for some years he had had symbolic dreams and symbolic hallucinations—as of a golden key, a tongue of flame, and voices— which had at the time baffled his understanding, but which he now interpreted as premonitory warnings that God had set him apart for a great mission. He remembered too that when still a child his mind had been engrossed by thoughts of God, and that in talking with his parents he had uttered words which caused them to declare that the angels spoke through his mouth. Remembering all these things, he could no longer doubt that Divinity had actually visited him in his humble London boarding house, and he made up his mind that he must bestir himself to carry out the divine command of expounding to his fellow men the hidden meaning of Holy Writ.

Forthwith, being still fired with the true scientist's passion for original research, he set himself to the task of learning Hebrew. He was, it will be remembered, approaching sixty, an age when the acquisition of a new language is exceedingly difficult and rare. Yet such progress did he make that within a very few months he was writing notes in explanation of the book of Genesis. And thus he continued not for months but years, patiently traversing the entire Bible, and at the same time carefully committing to paper everything "seen and heard" in the spiritual world; for his London excursion beyond the borderland which separates the here from the hereafter had been only the first of similar journeys taken not merely by night but in broad daylight. To use his own phraseology: "The Lord opened daily, very often, my bodily eyes; so that in the middle of the day I could see into the other world, and in a state of perfect wakefulness converse with angels and spirits."

His increasing absorption—absent-mindedness, his friends would call it—his habit of falling into trances, and his claim to interworld communication, could not fail to excite the surprise of all who had known him as scientist and philosopher. But these vagaries, as people deemed them, met the greater toleration because of the evident fact that they did not dim his intellectual powers and did not interfere with his activities in behalf of the public good. True, in 1747 he resigned his office of assessor of mines in order to have more leisure to prosecute his adventures into the unknown; but as a member of the Swedish Diet he continued to play a prominent part in the affairs of the Kingdom, giving long and profound study to the critical problems of administration, economics, and finance with which the nation's leaders were confronted during the third quarter of the century. So that— bearing in mind the further fact that he was no blatant advocate of his opinions— it seems altogether likely his spiritistic ideas would have gained no great measure of attention, had it not been for a series of singular occurrences that took place between 1759 and 1762.

Toward the end of July in the first of these years, Swedenborg (whose fondness for travel ceased only with his death) arrived in Gottenburg homeward bound from England, and on the invitation of a friend decided to break his journey by spending a few days in that city. Two hours after his arrival, while attending a small reception given in his honor, he electrified the company by abruptly declaring that at that moment a dangerous fire had broken out at Stockholm, three hundred miles away, and was spreading rapidly. Becoming excited, he rushed from the room, to reënter with the news that the house of one of his friends was in ashes, and that his own house was threatened. Anxious moments passed, while he restlessly paced up and down, in and out. Then, with a cry of joy, he exclaimed, "Thank God the fire is out, the third door from my house!"

Like wild the tidings spread through Gottenburg, and the greatest commotion prevailed. Some were inclined to give credence to Swedenborg's statements; more, who did not know the man, derided him as a sensation monger. But all had to wait with what patience they could, for those were the days before steam engine and telegraph. Forty-eight anxious hours passed. Then letters were received confirming the philosopher's announcement, and, we are assured, showing that the fire had taken precisely the path described by him, and had stopped where he had indicated.

No peace now for Swedenborg. His home at Stockholm, with its quaint gambrel roof, its summer houses, its neat flower beds, its curious box trees, instantly became a Mecca for the inquisitive, burning to see the man who held converse with the dead and was instructed by the latter in many portentous secrets. Most of those who gained admission, and through him sought to be put into touch with departed friends, received a courteous but firm refusal, accompanied by the explanation: "God having for wise and good purposes separated the world of spirits from ours, a communication is never granted without cogent reasons." When, however, his visitors satisfied him that they were imbued with something more than curiosity, he made an effort to meet their wishes, and occasionally with astonishing results.

It was thus in the case of Madam Marteville, widow of the Dutch Ambassador to Sweden. In 1761, some months after her husband's death, a goldsmith demanded from her payment for a silver service the Ambassador had bought from him. Feeling sure that the bill had already been paid, she made search for the receipt, but could find none. The sum involved was large, and she sought Swedenborg and asked him to seek her husband in the world of spirits and ascertain whether the debt had been settled. Three days later, when she was entertaining some friends, Swedenborg called, and in the most matter of fact way stated that he had had a conversation with Marteville, and had learned from him that the debt had been canceled seven months before his death, and that the receipt would be found in a certain bureau.

"But I have searched all through it," protested Madam Marteville.

"Ah," was Swedenborg's rejoinder; "but it has a secret drawer of which you know nothing."

At once all present hurried to the bureau, and there, in the private compartment which he quickly located, lay the missing receipt.

In similar fashion did Swedenborg relate to the Queen of Sweden, Louisa Ulrica, the substance of the last interview between her and her dead brother, the Crown Prince of Prussia, an interview which had been strictly private, and the subject of which, she affirmed, was such that no third person could possibly have known what passed between them.

More startling still was his declaration to a merry company at Amsterdam that at that same hour, in far away Russia, the Emperor Peter III. was being foully done to death in prison. Once more time proved that the spirit seer, as Swedenborg was now popularly known, had told the truth.

A decade more, and again we meet him in London, his whole being, at eighty-four, animated with the same energy and enthusiasm that had led him to seek and attain in his earlier manhood such a vast store of knowledge. And here, as Christmas drew near, he found lodging with two old friends, a wig maker and his wife. But ere Christmas dawned he lay a helpless victim of that dread disease paralysis. Not a word, not a movement, for full three weeks.

Then, with returning consciousness, a call for pen and paper. He would, he muttered with thickened speech, send a note to inform a certain John Wesley that the spirits had made known to him Wesley's desire to meet him, and that he would be glad to receive a visit at any time. In reply came word that the great evangelist had indeed wished to make the great mystic's acquaintance, and that after returning from a six months' circuit he would give himself the pleasure of waiting upon Swedenborg. "Too late," was the aged philosopher's comment as the story goes, "too late; for on the 29th of March I shall be in the world of spirits never more to return."

March came and went, and with it went his soul on the day predicted, if prediction there were. They buried him in London, and there in early season, out of his grave blossomed the religion that has preserved his name, his fame, his doctrines. To the dead Swedenborg succeeded the living Swedenborgianism.

But what shall those of us who are not Swedenborgians think of the master? Shall we accept at face value the story of his life as gathered from the documents left behind him and as set forth here; and, accepting it, believe that he was in reality a man set apart by God and granted the rare favor of insight into that unknown world to which all of us must some day go?

The true explanation, it seems to me, can be had only when we view Swedenborg in the light of the marvelous discoveries made during the last few years in the field of abnormal psychology. Beginning in France, and continuing more recently in the United States and other countries, investigations have been set on foot resulting in the solution of many human problems not unlike the riddle of Swedenborg, and occasionally far more complicated than that presented in his case. All these solutions, in the last analysis, rest on the basic discovery that human personality is by no means the single indivisible entity it is commonly supposed to be, but is instead singularly unstable and singularly complex. It has been found that under some unusual stimulus—such as an injury, an illness, or the strain of an intense emotion—there may result a disintegration, or, as it is technically termed, a dissociation, of personality, giving rise it may be to hysteria, it may be to hallucinations, it may even be to a complete disappearance of the original personality and its replacement by a new personality, sometimes of radically different characteristics.

It has also been found, by another group of investigators working principally in England, that side by side with the original, the waking, personality of everyday life, there coexists a hidden personality possessing faculties far transcending those enjoyed by the waking personality, but as a rule coming into play only at moments of crisis, though by some favored mortals invocable more frequently.

To this hidden personality, as distinguished from the secondary personality of dissociation, has been given the name of the subliminal self, and to its operation some attribute alike the productions of men of genius and the phenomena of clairvoyance and thought transference that have puzzled mankind from time immemorial.

Now, arguing by analogy from the cases scattered through the writings of Janet, Sidis, Prince, Myers, Gurney, and many others whose works the reader may consult for himself in any good public library, it is my belief that in Swedenborg we have a preëminent illustration both of dissociation and of subliminal action, and that it is therefore equally unnecessary to stigmatize him as insane or to adopt the spiritistic hypothesis in explanation of his utterances. The records show that from his father he inherited a tendency to hallucinations, checked for a time by the nature of his studies, but fostered as these expanded into pursuit of the absolute and the infinite. They further show that for a long time before the London visions he was in a disturbed state of health, his nervous system unstrung, his whole being so unhinged that at times he suffered from attacks of what was probably hystero-epilepsy.

It seems altogether likely, then, that in London the process of dissociation, after this period of gradual growth, suddenly leaped into activity. Thereafter his hallucinations, from being sporadic and vague, became habitual and definite, his hystero-epileptic attacks more frequent. But, happily for him, the dissociation never became complete. He was left in command of his original personality, his mental powers continued unabated; and he was still able to adjust himself to the environment of the world about him.

But, it may be objected, how explain his revelations in the matter of the fire at Stockholm, the missing receipt, the message to Queen Ulrica, and the death of Peter III.? This brings us to the question of subliminal action. Swedenborg himself, far in advance of his generation in this as in much else, appears to have realized that there was no need of invoking spirits to account for such transactions. "I need not mention," he once wrote, "the manifest sympathies acknowledged to exist in this lower world, and which are too many to be recounted; so great being the sympathy and magnetism of man that communication often takes place between those who are miles apart."

Here, in language that admits of no misinterpretation, we see stated the doctrine of telepathy, which is only now beginning to find acceptance among scientific men, but which, as I view it, has been amply demonstrated by the experiments of recent years and by the thousands of cases of spontaneous occurrence recorded in such publications as the "Proceedings of the Society for Psychical Research." And if these experiments and spontaneous instances prove anything, they prove that telepathy is distinctively a faculty of the subliminal self; and that a greater or less degree of dissociation is essential, not to the receipt, but to the objective realization, of telepathic messages. Thus, the entranced "medium" of modern days extracts from the depths of his sitter's subconsciousness facts which the sitter has consciously forgotten, facts even of which he may never have been consciously aware, but which have been transmitted telepathically to his subliminal self by the subliminal self of some third person.

So with Swedenborg. Admitting the authenticity of the afore-mentioned anecdotes—none of which, it is as well to point out, reaches us supported by first-hand evidence—it is quite unnecessary to appeal to spirits as his purveyors of knowledge. In every instance telepathy—or clairvoyance, which is after all explicable itself only by telepathy—will suffice. In the Marteville affair, for example, it is not unreasonable to assume that before his death the Ambassador telepathically told his devoted wife of the existence of the secret drawer and its contents; if, indeed, she had not known and forgotten. It would then be an exceedingly simple matter for the dissociated Swedenborg to acquire the desired information from the wife's subconsciousness. Nor does this reflect on his honesty. Doubtless he believed, as he represented, that he had actually had a conversation with the dead Marteville, and had learned from him the whereabouts of the missing receipt. In the form his dissociation took he could no more escape such a hallucination than can the twentieth-century medium avoid the belief that he is a veritable intermediary between the visible and the invisible world.

Not that I would put Swedenborg on a par with the ordinary medium. He was unquestionably a man of gigantic intellect, and he was unquestionably inspired, if by inspiration be understood the gift of combining subliminal with supraliminal powers to a degree granted to few of those whom the world counts truly great. If his fanciful and fantastic pictures of life in heaven and hell and in our neighboring planets welled up from the depths of his inmost mind, far more did the noble truths to which he gave expression. It is by these he should be judged; it is in these, not in his hallucinations nor in his telepathic exhibitions, that lies the secret of the commanding, if not always recognized, influence he has exercised on the thought of posterity. A solitary figure? True: but a grand figure, even in his saddest moment of delusion.

V

THE COCK LANE GHOST

The quaint old London church of St. Sepulchre's could not by any stretch of the imagination be called a fashionable place of worship. It stood in a crowded quarter of the city, and the gentry were content to leave it to the small tradesfolk and humble working people who made up its parish. Now and again a stray antiquarian paid it a fleeting visit; but, speaking generally, the coming of a stranger was so rare as to be accounted an event.

It is easy, then, to understand the sensation occasioned by the appearance at prayers one morning, in the year of grace, 1759, of a young and well dressed couple whose natural habitat was obviously in quite other surroundings. As they waited in the aisle—the man tall, erect, and easy of bearing, the woman fair and graceful—there was an instant craning of necks and vast nudging of one's neighbor; and long after they had seated themselves a subdued whispering bore further, if unnecessary, testimony to the curiosity they had aroused.

Probably no one felt a more lively interest than did the parish clerk, who, in showing them to a pew, had noted the tenderness with which they regarded each other. It needed nothing more to persuade him that they were eloping lovers, and that a snug gratuity was as good as in his pocket. All through the service he fidgeted impatiently in the shadows near the door, and as soon as the congregation was dismissed and he perceived that the visitors were lingering in their places, he hurried forward and accosted them. His name, he volubly explained, was Parsons; he was officiating clerk of the parish; likewise master in the charity school nearby. No doubt they would like to inspect the church, perhaps to visit the school; it might even be they were desirous of meeting the pastor? He would be delighted if he could serve them in any way.

"Possibly you can," said the man, "for you doubtless know the neighborhood like a book. My name is Knight, and this lady is my wife. We—" He stopped short at sight of the changed expression on the other's face, and breesquely demanded, "How now, man? What are you gaping at?"

"No offense, sir, no offense," stammered the disappointed and embarrassed clerk. "I beg your pardon, sir and madam."

There was an awkward pause before the man began again. "As I was saying, my name is Knight and this lady is my wife. We have only recently come to London and are in search of lodgings. If you know of any good place to which you can recommend us, we shall be heartily obliged to you."

Whatever he was, Clerk Parsons was not a fool, and these few words showed him plainly that he was face to face with a mystery. Elopers or no, such a well born couple would not from choice bury themselves in this forbidding section of London. With a cunning fostered by long years of precarious livelihood, he at once resolved to profit if he could from their need.

"I fear, sir," said he, "that I know of no lodgings that would be at all suitable for you. We are poor folk, all of us, and—"

"If you are honest folk," interrupted the lady, with an enchanting smile, "we ask no more."

Her husband checked her with a gesture and a look that was not lost on the now all-observing clerk, though it was long before he understood its significance.

"We are willing to pay a reasonable charge, and shall require only a bed-room and a sitting-room. If possible, we should prefer to be where there are no other lodgers."

"In that case," responded the clerk, with an eagerness he could scarcely veil, "I can accommodate you in my own house. It is simple but commodious, and I can answer that my wife will deal fairly by you."

"What think you, Fanny?" asked the man, turning to his wife.

"We can at least go and see."

This they immediately did, and to Clerk Parsons's joy decided to make their home with him. Nor did their coming gladden the clerk alone. His wife and children, two little girls of nine and ten, from the moment they saw the "beautiful lady" conceived a warm attachment for her. Her geniality, her kindliness, her manifest love for her husband, appealed to their sympathies, as did the sadness which from time to time clouded her face. If, like Parsons himself, they soon became convinced that she and her husband shared some momentous secret, they could not bring themselves to believe that it involved her in wrongdoing. For the husband too they entertained the friendliest feelings. He was of a blunt, outspoken disposition and perhaps a trifle quick tempered, but he was frank and liberal and sincerely devoted to his wife. For all in the household, therefore, the days passed pleasantly; and when Mrs. Parsons one fine spring morning discovered her fair guest in tears she felt that time had established between them relations sufficiently confidential to warrant her motherly intervention.

"Come, my dear," said she, "I have long seen that something is troubling you. Tell me what it is, that I may be able to comfort, perhaps aid you."

"It is nothing, good Mrs. Parsons, nothing. I am very foolish. I was thinking of what would become of me if anything should happen to my husband."

"Dear, dear! and nothing will. But you could then turn to your relatives."

"I have no relatives."

"What, my dear, are they all dead?"

"No," in a solemn tone, "but I am dead to them."

In a voice shaken by sobs, she now unfolded her story, and pitiful enough it was. She was, it appeared, the sister of Knight's first wife, who had died in Norfolk leaving a new born child that survived its mother only a few hours. At Knight's request she then went to keep house for him, and presently they found themselves very much in love with each other. But in the canon law they discovered an insuperable obstacle to marriage. Had the wife died without issue, or had her child not been born alive, the law would have permitted her, even though a "deceased wife's sister," to wed the man of her choice. As things stood, a legitimate union was out of the question. Learning this, they resolved to separate; but separation brought only increased longing. Thence grew a rapid and mutual persuasion that, under the circumstances, it would be no sin to bid defiance to the canon law and live together as man and wife. This view not finding favor with their relatives, and becoming apprehensive of arrest and imprisonment, they had fled to London and had hidden themselves in its depths. Surely, she concluded, with a desperate intensity, surely fair-minded people would not condemn them; surely all who knew what true love was would feel that they could not have acted otherwise?

This confession, though it did not in the least diminish her landlady's regard for her, worked indirectly in a most disastrous way. Whether driven by necessity, or emboldened by the belief that his lodgers were at his mercy, the clerk soon afterward approached Knight for a small loan; and, obtaining it, repeated the request on several other occasions, until he had borrowed in all about twelve pounds. Payment he postponed on one pretext and another, until the lender finally lost all patience and informed him roundly that he must settle or stand suit. Then followed an interchange of words that in an instant terminated the pleasant connection of the preceding months. Parsons was described as "an impudent scoundrel who would be taught what honesty meant." Parsons described himself as "knowing what honesty meant full well, and needing no lessons from a fugitive from justice." White with rage, Knight bundled his belongings together, called a hackney coach, and within the hour had shaken the dust of Cock Lane from his feet, finding new lodgings in Clerkenwell and at once haling his whilom landlord to the debtors' court.

A little time, and all else was forgotten in the serious illness of his beloved Fanny. At first the physician declared that the malady would prove slight; but she herself seemed to feel that she was doomed. "Send for a lawyer," she urged; "I want to make my will. It is little enough I have, God knows; but I wish to be sure you will get it all, dear husband."

To humor her, the will was drawn, and now it developed that the disease which had attacked her was smallpox in its worst form. No need to dwell on the fearful hours that followed, the fond farewells, the lapsing into a merciful unconsciousness, the death. They buried her in the vaults of St. John's Clerkenwell, and from her tomb her husband came forth to give battle to the relatives who, shunning her while alive, did not disdain to seek possession of the small legacy she had left him. In this they failed, but scarcely had the smoke of the legal canonading cleared away, before he was called upon to meet a new issue so unexpected and so mysterious that history affords no stranger sequel to tale of love.

The first intimation of its coming and of its nature was revealed to him, as to the public generally, by a brief paragraph printed in a mid January, 1762, issue of *The London Ledger.*

"For some time past a great knocking having been heard in the night, at the officiating parish clerk's of St. Sepulchre's, in Cock Lane near Smithfield, to the great terror of the family, and all means used to discover the meaning of it, four gentlemen sat up there last Friday night, among whom was a clergyman standing withinside the door, who asked various questions. On his asking whether any one had been murdered, no answer was made; but on his asking whether any one had been poisoned, it knocked one and thirty times. The report current in the neighborhood is that a woman was some time ago poisoned, and buried at St. John's Clerkenwell, by her brother-in-law."

Instantly the city was agog, and for the next fortnight *The Ledger*, *The Chronicle*, and other newspapers gave much of their space to details of the pretended revelations, though they were careful to refer to names by blanks or initials only. These accounts informed their readers that the knocking had first been heard in the life time of the deceased when, during the absence of her supposed husband, she had shared her bed with Clerk Parsons's oldest daughter; that she had then pronounced it an omen of her early death; that it did not occur again until after she had died; that, if the soi-disant spirit could be believed, the earlier knocking had been due to the agency of her dead sister; and that, in her own turn, she had come back to bring to justice the villain who had murdered her for the little she possessed. In commenting on this amazing story, the papers were prompt to point out that the knocking was heard only in the presence of the afore-mentioned daughter, now a girl of twelve; and while one or two, like *The Ledger*, inclined to credence, the majority followed *The Chronicle* in denouncing the affair as an "imposture."

The outraged husband, as may be imagined, lost not a moment in demanding admission to the séances which were proceeding merrily under the direction of a servant in the Parsons family and a clergyman of the neighborhood. He found that the method practised was to put the girl to bed, wait until the knocking should begin, and then question the alleged spirit; when answers were received according to a code of one knock for an affirmative and two knocks for a negative. It was in his presence, then, though not at a single sitting, that the following dialogue was in this way carried on:

"Are you Miss Fanny?"—"Yes."

"Did you die naturally?"—"No."

"Did you die by poison?"—"Yes."

"Do you know what kind of poison it was?"—"Yes."

"Was it arsenic?"—"Yes."

"Was it given to you by any person other than Mr. Knight?"—"No."

"Do you wish that he be hanged?"—"Yes."

"Was it given to you in gruel?"—"No."

"In beer?"—"Yes."

Here a spectator interrupted with the remark that the deceased was never known to drink beer, but had been fond of purl, and the question was hastily put:

"Was it not in purl?"—"Yes."

"How long did you live after taking it?"—Three knocks, held to mean three hours.

"Did Carrots" (her maid) "know of your being poisoned?"—"Yes."

"Did you tell her?"—"Yes."

"How long was it after you took it before you told her?" One knock, for one hour.

Here was something tangible, and Knight went to work with a will to refute the terrible charge brought by the invisible accuser. As reported in *The Daily Gazetteer*, which had promised that "the reader may expect to be enlightened from time to time to the utmost of our power in this intricate and dark affair," the maid Carrots was found, and from her was procured a sworn statement that Mrs. Knight had said not a word to her about being poisoned; that, indeed, she had become unconscious twelve hours before her death and remained unconscious to the end. The physician and apothecary who had attended her made affidavit to the same effect, and described the fatal nature of her illness. It was further shown that her death at most benefited Knight by not more than a hundred pounds, of which he had no need, as he was of independent means.

Altogether, he would seem to have cleared himself effectually. Still the knocking continued, and night after night the accusation was repeated. He now resorted, therefore, to a radical step to convince the public that he was the victim of a monstrous fraud.

Asserting that little Miss Parsons herself produced the mysterious sounds, and that she did so at the instigation of her father, he secured an order for her removal to the house of a friend of his, a Clerkenwell clergyman. Here a decisive failure was recorded against the ghost. It had promised that it would knock on the coffin containing Mrs. Knight's remains; and about one o'clock in the morning, after hours of silent watching, during which the spirit gave not a sign of its presence, the entire company adjourned to the church. Only one member was found of sufficient boldness to plunge with Knight into the gloomy depths where the dead lay entombed; and that one bore out his statement that never a knock had been heard. The girl was urged to confess, but persisted in her assertions that the ghost was in nowise of her making.

Afterward, when the knocking had been resumed under more favorable auspices, word came from the unseen world that the fiasco in the church was ascribable to the very good reason that Knight had caused his wife's coffin to be secretly removed. "I will show them!" cried the desperate man. With clergyman, sexton, and undertaker, he visited the vaults once more and not only identified but opened the coffin.

Meanwhile all London was flocking to Cock Lane as to a raree-show, on foot, on horseback, in vehicles of every description. Some, like the celebrated Dr. Johnson who took part in the coffin opening episode in Clerkenwell, were animated by scientific zeal; but idle curiosity inspired the great majority. The gossiping Walpole, in a letter to his friend Montagu, has left a graphic picture of the stir created by the newspaper reports.

"I went to hear it," he writes; "for it is not an apparition but an audition. We set out from the opera, changed our clothes at Northumberland House, the Duke of York, Lady Northumberland, Lady Mary Coke, Lord Hertford, and I, all in one hackney coach, and drove to the spot; it rained in torrents; yet the lane was full of mob, and the house so full we could not get in; at last they discovered it was the Duke of York, and the company squeezed themselves into one another's pockets to make room for us. The house, which is borrowed, and to which the ghost has adjourned, is wretchedly small and miserable; when we opened the chamber, in which were fifty people with no light but one tallow candle at the end, we tumbled over the bed of the child to whom the ghost comes, and whom they are murdering by inches in such insufferable heat and stench. At the top of the room are clothes to dry. I asked if we were to have rope dancing between the acts. We heard nothing; they told us (as they would at a puppet show) that it would not come that night till seven in the morning, that is, when there are only prentices and old women. We stayed, however, till half an hour after one."

The skepticism patent in this letter was shared by all thinking men. Letter after letter of criticism, even of abuse, was poured into the newspapers. No less a personage than Oliver Goldsmith wrote, under the title of "The Mystery Revealed," a long pamphlet which was intended both to explain away the disturbances and to defend the luckless Knight. The actor Garrick dragged into a prologue a riming and sneering reference to the mystery; the artist Hogarth invoked his genius to deride it. Yet there were believers in plenty, and there even seem to have been some who thought of preying on the credulous by opening up a business in "knocking ghosts."

"On Tuesday last," one reads in *The Chronicle*, "it was given out that a new knocking ghost was to perform that evening at a house in Broad Court near Bow Street, Covent Garden; information of which being given to a certain magistrate in the neighborhood, he sent his compliments with an intimation that it should not meet with that lenity the Cock Lane ghost did, but that it should knock hemp in Bridewell. On which the ghost very discreetly omitted the intended exhibition."

Whether or no he took a hint from this publication, it is certain that, finding all other means failing, Knight now resolved to try to lay by legal process the ghost that had rendered him the most unhappy and the most talked of man in London. Going before a magistrate, he brought a charge of criminal conspiracy against Clerk Parsons, Mrs. Parsons, the Parsons servant, the clergyman who had aided the servant in eliciting the murder story from the talkative ghost, and a Cock Lane tradesman. All of these, he alleged, had banded themselves together to ruin him, their malice arising from the quarrel which had led him to remove to Clerkenwell and enter a lawsuit against Parsons. The girl herself he did not desire punished, because she was too young to understand the evil that she wrought.

Warrants were forthwith issued, and, protesting their innocence frantically, the accused were dragged to prison.

Their conviction soon followed, after a trial of which the only obtainable evidence is that it was held at the Guildhall before a special jury and was presided over by Lord Mansfield. Then, "the court desiring that Mr. K——, who had been so much injured on this occasion, should receive some reparation," sentence was deferred for several months. This enabled the clergyman and the tradesman "to purchase their pardon" by the payment of some five hundred or six hundred pounds to Knight. But the clerk either would not or could not pay a farthing, and on him and his, sentence was now passed. "The father," to quote once more from the meager account in *The Annual Register*, "was ordered to be set in the pillory three times in one month, once at the end of Cock Lane, and after that to be imprisoned two years; Elizabeth his wife, one year; and Mary Frazer, six months to Bridewell, and to be kept there to hard labor." Thus, in wig and gown, did the law solemnly and severely place the seal of disbelief on the Cock Lane ghost; which, it is worth observing, seems to have vanished forever the moment the arrests were made.

But, looking back at the case from the vantage point of chronological distance and of recent research into kindred affairs, it is difficult to accept as final the verdict reached by the "special jury" and concurred in by the public opinion of the day. It is preposterous to suppose that for so slight a cause as a dispute over twelve pounds Clerk Parsons and his associates would conspire to ruin a man's reputation and if possible to take his life; and still more preposterous to imagine that they would adopt such a means to attain this end. Of course, they may have had stronger reasons for being hostile to Knight than appears from the published facts. Yet it is significant that when the clerk was placed in the pillory he seemed to "be out of his mind," and so evident was his misery that the assembled mob "instead of using him ill, made a handsome collection for him."

The more likely, nay the only defensible solution of the problem, is that he, his fellow sufferers, and Knight himself were one and all the victims of the uncontrollable impulses of a hysterical child. The case bears too strong a resemblance to the Tedworth and Epworth disturbances to admit of any other hypothesis. Not that the Parsons girl is to be placed on exactly the same footing as the Mompesson children and Hetty Wesley, and held to some extent responsible for the mischievous phenomena she produced.

On the contrary, the more one studies the evidence the stronger grows the conviction that in her we have a striking and singular instance of "dissociation." She was, it is very evident, strongly attached to the unfortunate Mrs. Knight, doubtless felt keenly the separation from her, and, whether consciously or subconsciously, would cherish a grudge against Knight as the cause of that separation. The news of Mrs. Knight's death would come as a great shock, and might easily act, so to speak, as the fulcrum of the lever of mental disintegration. Then, dimly enough at first but soon with portentous rapidity, her disordered consciousness would conceive the idea that her friend had been murdered and that it was her duty to bring the slayer to justice. From this it would be an easy step to the development, in the neurotic child, of a full fledged secondary personality, akin to that found in the spiritistic mediums of later times.

Now, for the first time, her faculties would seem to her astonished parents to be in the keeping and under the control of an extraneous being, a departed, discarnate spirit; and in this error she and they would be confirmed by the suggestions and foolish questions of those who came to marvel. It needed another great shock—there being in those days no Janet or Prince or Sidis to take charge of the case—the shock of the arrest and imprisonment of her parents, to effect at least partial reintegration and the consequent disappearance of the secondary self, the much debated, malevolent Cock Lane ghost.

VI

THE GHOST SEEN BY LORD BROUGHAM

It is comparatively easy, when seated before a roaring fire in a well-lighted room, to sneer ghosts out of existence, and roundly affirm that they are without exception the fanciful products of a heated imagination. But the matter takes on a very different complexion, when in that same room and without so much as the opening of a door, one is unexpectedly confronted by the figure of an absent friend, who, it subsequently appears, is about that time breathing his last in another part of the world. Especially would it seem impossible to remain skeptical if there existed between oneself and the friend in question a compact, drawn up years before in an access of youthful enthusiasm, binding whichever should die first to appear to the other at the moment of death.

This, as all students of ghostology are aware, has frequently been the case; and it was precisely the case with the ghost seen by the famous Lord Brougham, the brilliant and versatile Scotchman, whose astonishingly long and successful career in England as statesman, judge, lawyer, man of science, philanthropist, orator, and author won him a place among the immortals both of the Georgian and of the Victorian era.

At the time he saw the ghost he was still a young man, thinking far less of what the future might hold than of the pleasures of the present. In fact, it is difficult to imagine a more unlikely subject for a ghostly experience. From his earliest youth, his father, a most matter of fact person, sedulously endeavored to impress him with the belief that the only spirits deserving of the name were those which came in oddly labeled bottles; and in support of this view the elder Brougham frequently related the adventures of sundry persons of his acquaintance who had engaged in the mischievous pastime of ghost hunting. Added to the natural effect of such tales as these was the inherent exuberance of Brougham's disposition and the bent of his mind to mathematics and kindred exact sciences.

It was at the Edinburgh high school that he first met his future ghost, who at the time was a youngster like himself, and became and long remained his most intimate friend. The two lads were graduated together from the high school, and together matriculated into the university, where, in the intervals Brougham could spare from his favorite studies and recreations, and from the company of the daredevil students with whom he soon began to associate, they continued their old time walks and talks.

On one of these walks, the conversation happened to turn to the perennial problem of life beyond the grave and the possibility of the dead communicating with the living. Brougham, mindful of the views maintained by his father, doubtless treated the subject lightly, if not scoffingly; but one word led to another, until finally, in what he afterward described as a moment of folly, he covenanted with his friend that whichever of them should happen to pass from earth first would, if it were at all possible, show himself in spirit to the other, and thus prove beyond peradventure that the soul of man survived the death of the body.

So far as Brougham was concerned, this undertaking was speedily forgotten in the pressure of the many activities into which he plunged with all the ardor of his impetuous nature. His days were given wholly to the pursuit of knowledge; his nights to the pursuit of pleasure, as pleasure was then counted by the roystering young Scotchmen, whose favorite resort was the tavern, and whose most popular pastime was filching signs, bell handles, and knockers, and stirring the city guard to unwonted energy. Under such conditions neither the death pact nor the solemn minded youth with whom he had made it could remain long in his memory; and it is not surprising to find that with the end of college life and the removal of his boyhood's friend to India, where he entered the civil service, they soon became as strangers to each other.

Brougham himself remained in Edinburgh to read for the law, and incidentally to develop with the aid of an amateur debating society the oratorical talents that were in time to make him the logical successor of Pitt, Fox, and Burke in the House of Commons. He continued none the less a lover of pleasure, some of which, however, he now took in the healthy form of long walking trips through the Highlands. In this way he acquired a desire for travel, and when, in the autumn of 1799, an opportunity came for an extended tour of Denmark, Sweden, and Norway, he grasped it eagerly. Together with the future diplomat, Lord Stuart of Rothsay, then plain Charles Stuart and the boon companion of many a pedestrian excursion, he sailed for Copenhagen late in September, and by leisurely stages made his way thence to Stockholm, alive to all the varied interests of the novel scenes in which he found himself; but encountering little that was exciting or adventurous, until, after a prolonged sojourn in the Swedish capital and a brief visit to Göteborg, he started for Norway.

By this time the weather had turned so cold that the travelers resolved to bring their tour to a sudden end, and to press on as rapidly as the bad roads would permit to some Norwegian port, where they hoped to find a ship that would carry them back to Scotland. Accordingly, leaving Göteborg early in the morning of December 19, they journeyed steadily until after midnight, when they came to an inn that seemed to promise comfortable sleeping accommodations. Stuart lost no time in going to bed; but Brougham decided to wait until a hot bath could be prepared for him.

Plunging into it, and forgetful of everything save the warmth that was doubly welcome after the cold of the long drive, he suddenly became aware that he was not alone in the room. No door had opened, not a footstep had been heard; but in the light of the flickering candles he plainly saw the figure of a man seated in the chair on which he had carelessly thrown his clothes. And this figure he instantly recognized as that of his early playmate, the forgotten chum who, as he well knew, had years before gone from the land of the heather to the land of the blazing sun. Yet here he sat, in the quaintly furnished sleeping chamber of a Swedish roadside inn, gazing composedly at his astounded friend. At once there flashed into Brougham's mind remembrance of the death pact, and he leaped from the bath, only to lose all consciousness and fall headlong to the floor. When he revived, the apparition had disappeared.

There was little sleep for the hard headed Scotchman that night. The vision had been too definite, the shock too intense. But, dressing, he sat down and strove to debate the matter in the light of cold reason. He must, he argued, have dozed off in the bath and experienced a strange dream. To be sure, he had not been thinking of his old comrade, and for years had had no communication with him. Nor had anything taken place during the tour to bring to memory either him or any member of his family, or to turn Brougham's mind to thoughts of India. Still, he found it impossible to believe that he had seen a ghost. At most, he reiterated to himself, it could have been nothing more than an exceptionally clear cut dream. And to this opinion he stubbornly adhered, notwithstanding the receipt, soon after his return to Edinburgh, of a letter from India announcing the death of the friend who had been so mysteriously recalled to his recollection, and giving December 19 as the date of death. More than sixty years later we find him, in his autobiography commenting on the experience anew, granting that it was a strange coincidence but refusing to admit that it was anything more than the coincidence of a dream.

It was in his autobiography, by the way, that he first referred to the confirmatory letter. This fact, taken in connection with his reputation for holding the truth in light esteem and with several vague and puzzling statements contained in the detailed account of the experience itself as set forth in his journal of the Scandinavian tour, has led some critics to make the suggestion that his narrative partakes of the nature of fiction rather than of a sober recital of facts. Against this, however, must be set Brougham's complete and invincible repugnance to accept at face value anything bordering on the supernatural. He took no pleasure in the thought that he had possibly been the recipient of a visit from a departed spirit. On the contrary, it annoyed him, and he sought earnestly to find a natural explanation for an occurrence which remained unique throughout his long life. No one would have been readier to point out the futility of the apparition if the absent friend had really continued hale and hearty after December 19. And it is therefore reasonable to assume that had he wished to falsify at all, he would have given an altogether different sequel to the story of his vision or dream, as he preferred to call it, though the evidence which he himself furnishes shows that he was not asleep.

The question still remains, of course, whether he was justified in dismissing it as a sheer chance coincidence. If it stood by itself, it would obviously be permissible to accept this explanation as all sufficient. But the fact is that it is only one of many similar instances. This was strikingly brought out only a few years ago through a far reaching inquiry, a "census of hallucinations," instituted by a special committee of the Society for Psychical Research.

Enlisting the services of some four hundred "collectors," the committee instructed each of these to address to twenty-five adults, selected at random, the query, "Have you ever, when believing yourself to be completely awake, had a vivid impression of seeing or being touched by a living being or inanimate object, or of hearing a voice; which impression, so far as you could discover, was not due to any external physical cause?" In all, seventeen thousand people were thus questioned, and almost ten per cent. of the answers received proved to be in the affirmative. More than this, it appeared that out of a total of three hundred and fifty recognized apparitions of living persons, no fewer than sixty-five were "death coincidences," in which the hallucinatory experience occurred within from one hour to twelve hours after the death of the person seen.

Sifting these death coincidences carefully, the committee for various reasons rejected more than half, and at the same time raised the total of recognized apparitions of living persons from three hundred and fifty to thirteen hundred. This was done in order to make generous allowance for the number of such apparitions forgotten by those to whom the question had been put, investigation showing that the great majority of hallucinations reported were given as of comparatively recent occurrence, and that there was a rapid decrease as the years of occurrence became more remote.

As a final result, therefore, the committee found about thirty death coincidences out of thirteen hundred cases, or a proportion of one in forty-three. Computing from the average annual death-rate for England and Wales, it was calculated that the probability that any one person would die on a given day was about one in nineteen thousand; in other words, out of every nineteen thousand apparitions of living persons, there should occur, by chance alone, one death coincidence. The actual proportion, however, as established by the inquiry, was equivalent to about four hundred and forty in nineteen thousand, or four hundred and forty times the most probable number, and this when the apparitions reported were considered merely collectively as having been seen at any time within twelve hours after death. Not a few, as a matter of fact, were reported as having been seen within one hour after death, and for these the improbability of occurrence by chance alone was manifestly twelve times four hundred and forty. In view of these considerations the committee felt warranted in declaring that "between deaths and apparitions of dying persons a connection exists which is not due to chance."

Had Lord Brougham lived to study the statistics of this remarkable census of hallucinations, he might have formed a higher opinion of his ghost; but he would also have been in a better position to deny its supernatural attributes. For, if the Society for Psychical Research has made it impossible to doubt the existence of such ghosts as that which he beheld during his travels in Sweden, it has likewise made discoveries which afford a really substantial reason for asserting that they no more hail from the world beyond than do ghosts that are unmistakably the creations of fancy or fraud. This results from the society's investigations of thought transference or telepathy, to use the term now commonly employed.

At an early stage of the experiments undertaken to determine the possibility of transmitting thought from mind to mind without the intervention of any known means of communication, it was found that when success attended the efforts of the experimenters the telepathic message was frequently received not in the form of pure thought but as a hallucinatory image; and what is still more important in the present connection, it was further found possible so to produce not merely images of cards, flowers, books, and other inanimate objects, but also images of living persons.

Thus, as chronicled with corroborative evidence in the society's "Proceedings," an English clergyman named Godfrey telepathically caused a distant friend to see an apparition of him one night; the same result was achieved by a Mr. Sinclair of New Jersey, who, during a visit to New York, succeeded in projecting a phantasm of himself which was clearly seen by his wife in Lakewood; and similarly a Mr. Kirk, while seated in his London office, paid a telepathic visit to the home of a young woman, who saw him as distinctly as though he had gone there in the flesh. In all of these, as in other cases recorded by the society, the persons to whom the apparitions were vouchsafed had no idea that any experiment of the kind was being attempted.

Indeed, there is on record an apparently well authenticated instance of the experimental production of an apparition not of the living but of the dead. This occurred in Germany many years ago, when a certain Herr Wesermann undertook to "will" a military friend into dreaming of a woman who had long been dead. The sequel may be related in Herr Wesermann's own words:

"A lady, who had been dead five years, was to appear to Lieutenant N. in a dream at 10.30 P.M., and incite him to good deeds. At half-past ten, contrary to expectation, Herr N. had not gone to bed but was discussing the French campaign with his friend Lieutenant S. in the ante-room. Suddenly the door of the room opened, the lady entered dressed in white, with a black kerchief and uncovered head, greeted S. with her hand three times in a friendly manner; then turned to N., nodded to him, and returned again through the doorway.

"As this story, related to me by Lieutenant N., seemed to be too remarkable from a psychological point of view for the truth of it not to be duly established, I wrote to Lieutenant S., who was living six miles away, and asked him to give me his account of it. He sent me the following reply:

"'On the thirteenth of March, 1817, Herr N. came to pay me a visit at my lodgings about a league from A———. He stayed the night with me. After supper, and when we were both undressed, I was sitting on my bed and Herr N. was standing by the door of the next room on the point also of going to bed. This was about half-past ten. We were speaking partly about indifferent subjects and partly about the events of the French campaign. Suddenly the door of the kitchen opened without a sound, and a lady entered, very pale, taller than Herr N., about five feet four inches in height, strong and broad of figure, dressed in white, but with a large black kerchief which reached to below the waist.

"'She entered with bare head, greeted me with the hand three times in complimentary fashion, turned round to the left toward Herr N., and waved her hand to him three times; after which the figure quietly, and again without any creaking of the door, went out. We followed at once in order to discover whether there were any deception, but found nothing. The strangest thing was this, that our night-watch of two men whom I had shortly found on the watch were now asleep, though at my first call they were on the alert; and that the door of the room, which always opens with a good deal of noise, did not make the slightest sound when opened by the figure.'"

It is also significant that, as was made evident by the census of hallucinations, by far the larger number of apparitions reported are those of persons still alive and well. In these cases, nobody being dead, it is absurd to raise the cry of spirits, and the only tenable hypothesis is that, through one of the several causes which seem to quicken telepathic action, a spontaneous telepathic hallucination has been produced. Now, the experiments conducted by the society and by independent investigators have shown that telepathic messages often lie dormant for hours beneath the threshold of the receiver's consciousness, being consciously apprehended only when certain favoring conditions arise; as, for example, when the receiver has fallen asleep, or into a state of reverie, or when, tired out after a long day's work, he has utterly relaxed mentally. This is technically known as "deferred percipience," and, considered in conjunction with the discoveries mentioned, it is amply sufficient to dislodge from the realm of the supernatural the ghost seen by Lord Brougham, and every ghost that is not a mere imposter.

In the Brougham case the exciting cause of the hallucination seems to have been the death pact. As he lay dying in India, the mind of the whilom schoolboy would, consciously or unconsciously, revert to that agreement with the friend of his youth, and thence would arise the desire to let him know that the plighted word had not been forgotten. Across the vast intervening space, by what mechanism we as yet do not know, the message would flash instantaneously, to remain unapprehended, perhaps for hours after the death of the sender, until, in the quiet of the Swedish inn and resting from the fatigues of the journey, Brougham's mental faculties passed momentarily into the condition necessary for its objective realization.

Then, precisely as in experimental telepathy the receiver sees a hallucinatory image of the trinket or the book; with a suddenness and vividness that could not fail to shock him, the message would find expression by the creation before Brougham's startled eyes of a hallucinatory image of the friend who, as he was to learn later, had died that same day thousands of miles from Sweden. Knowing nothing of the possibilities of the human mind, as revealed, if only faintly, by the labors of a later generation, it was inevitable he should believe he had no alternative between dismissing the experience as a peculiar dream or admitting that in very truth he had looked upon a ghost.

VII

THE SEERESS OF PREVORST

Modern spiritism, as every student of that fascinating if elusive subject is aware, dates from the closing years of the first half of the nineteenth century. But the celebrated Fox sisters, whose revelations at that time served to crystallize into an organized religious system the idea of the possibility of communication between this world and the world beyond, were by no means the first of spiritistic mediums. Long before their day there were those who professed to have cognizance of things unseen and to act as intermediaries between the living and the dead; and although lost to sight amid the throng of latter-day claimants to similar powers, the achievements of some of these early adventurers into the unknown have not been surpassed by the best performances of the Fox girls and their long line of successors.

Especially is this true of the mediumship of a young German woman, Frederica Hauffe, who in the course of her short, pitiful, and tragic career is credited with having displayed more varied and picturesque supernatural gifts than the most renowned wonder-worker of to-day. Like many modern mediums she was of humble origin, her birthplace being a forester's hut in the Würtemberg mountain village of Prevorst; and here, among wood-cutters and charcoal-burners, she passed the first years of her life. Even while still a child she seems to have attracted wide-spread attention on account of certain peculiarities of temperament and conduct. It was noticed that though naturally gay and playful she occasionally assumed a strangely intent and serious manner; that in her happiest moments she was subject to unaccountable fits of shuddering and shivering; and that she seemed keenly alive not merely to the sights and sounds of every-day life but to influences unfelt by those about her. This last trait received a sudden and unexpected development when, at the age of twelve or thirteen, she was sent to the neighboring town of Löwenstein to be educated under the care of her grand-parents, a worthy couple named Schmidgall.

Grandfather Schmidgall was an exceedingly superstitious old man, with a singular fondness for visiting solitary and gloomy places, particularly churchyards; and he soon began to take the little girl with him on such strolls. But he discovered, much to his amazement, that though she listened with avidity to the tales he told her of the romantic and mysterious events that had occurred within the somber ruins with which the countryside was liberally endowed, she was reluctant to explore those ruins or wander among the graves where he delighted to resort. At first he was inclined to ascribe her reluctance to weak and sentimental timidity, but he speedily found reason to adopt an altogether different view. He noticed that whenever he took her to graveyards or to churches in which there were graves, her frail form became greatly agitated, and at times she seemed rooted to the ground; and that there were certain places, especially an old kitchen in a nearby castle, which he could not persuade her to enter, and the mere sight of which caused her to quake and tremble. "The child," he told his wife, "feels the presence of the dead, and, mark you, she will end by seeing the dead."

He was, therefore, more alarmed than surprised when one midnight, long after he had fancied her in bed and asleep, she ran to his room and informed him that she had just beheld in the hall a tall, dark figure which, sighing heavily, passed her and disappeared in the vestibule. With awe, not unmixed with satisfaction, Schmidgall remembered that he had once seen the self-same apparition; but he prudently endeavored to convince her that she had been dreaming and sent her back to her room, which, thenceforward, he never allowed her to leave at night.

In this way Frederica Hauffe's mediumship began. But several years were to pass before she saw another ghost or gave evidence of possessing supernormal powers other than by occasional dreams of a prophetic and revelatory nature. In the meanwhile she rejoined her parents and moved with them from Prevorst to Oberstenfeld, where, in her nineteenth year, she was married. It was distinctly a marriage of convenience, arranged without regard to her wishes, and the moment the engagement was announced she secluded herself from her friends and passed her days and nights in weeping. For weeks together she went without sleep, ate scarcely anything, and became thin, pale, and feeble. It was rumored that she had set her affections in another quarter: but her relatives angrily denied this and asserted that once married she would soon become herself again.

They were mistaken. From her wedding day, which she celebrated by attending the funeral of a venerable clergyman to whom she had been warmly attached, her health broke rapidly. One morning she awoke in a high fever that lasted a fortnight and was followed by convulsive spasms, during which she beheld at the bedside the image of her grandmother Schmidgall, who, it subsequently developed, was at that moment dying in distant Löwenstein. The spasms continuing, despite the application of the customary rude remedies of the time, it was decided to send for a physician with some knowledge of mesmerism, which was then becoming popular in Germany. To the astonishment of those who thronged the sick room, the first touch of his hand on her forehead brought relief. The convulsions ceased, she became calm, and presently she fell asleep. But on awaking she was attacked as before, and try as he might the physician could not effect a permanent cure. To all his "passes" she responded with gratifying promptitude, only to suffer a relapse the moment she was released from the mesmeric influence.

At this juncture aid was received from a most extraordinary source, according to the story Frederica told her wondering friends. With benign visage and extended hand, the spirit of her grandmother appeared to her for seven successive nights, mesmerized her, and taught her how to mesmerize herself. The results of this visitation, if not altogether fortunate, were at least to some extent curative. There were periods when she was able not merely to leave her bed but to attend to household duties and indulge in long walks and drives. But it was painfully apparent that she was still in a precarious condition.

From her infancy she had always been powerfully affected by the touch of different metals, and now this phenomenon was intensified a thousand-fold. The placing of a magnet on her forehead caused her features to be contorted as though by a stroke of paralysis; contact with glass and sand made her cataleptic. Once she was found seated on a sandstone bench, unable to move hand or foot. About this time also she acquired the faculty of crystal-gazing; that is to say, by looking into a bowl of water she could correctly describe scenes transpiring at a distance. More than this, she now declared that behind the persons in whose company she was she perceived ghostly forms, some of which she recognized as dead acquaintances.

Unlike her grandmother, these new visitants from the unknown world did not provide her with the means of regaining her lost health. On the contrary, from the time they first put in their appearance she grew far worse, suffering not so much from convulsive attacks as from an increasing lassitude. She complained that eating was a great tax on her strength, and that rising and walking were out of the question. Unable to comprehend this new turn of affairs, her attendants lost all patience, declared that if she had made up her mind to die she might as well do so as at once, and tried to force her to leave her bed. Finally her parents intervened, and at their request she was brought back to Oberstenfeld.

Here she found an altogether congenial environment, and for a while showed marked improvement. Here too, and in a most sensational way, her mediumship blossomed into full fruition. She had been home for only a short time when the family began to be disturbed by mysterious noises for which they could find no cause. A sound like the ringing of glasses was frequently heard, as were footsteps and knockings on the walls. Her father, in particular, asserted that sometimes he felt a strange pressure on his shoulder or his foot. The impression grew that the house, which was part of the ancient, picturesque, and none too well preserved cathedral of Oberstenfeld, was haunted by the spirits of its former occupants.

One night, shortly after retiring to the room which they shared in common, Frederica, her sister, and a maid servant saw a lighted candle, apparently of its own volition, move up and down the table on which it was burning. The sister and the servant saw nothing more; but Frederica the next instant beheld a thin, grayish cloud, which presently resolved into the form of a man, about fifty years old, attired in the costume of a medieval knight. Approaching, this strange apparition gazed steadfastly at her, and in a low but clear tone urged her to rise and follow it, saying that she alone could loosen its bonds. Overcome with terror, she cried out that she would not follow, then ran across the room and hid herself in the bed where her sister and the servant lay panic-stricken. That night she saw no more of the apparition: but the maid, whom they sent to sleep in the bed she had so hurriedly vacated, declared that the coverings were forcibly drawn off her by an unseen hand.

The next night the apparition appeared to Frederica again, and to her alone. This time it seemed not sorrowful but angry, and threatened that if she did not rise and follow she would be hurled out of the window. At her bold retort, "In the name of Jesus, do it!" the apparition vanished, to return a few nights later, and after that to show itself to her by day as well as by night.

It now informed her that it was the ghost of a nobleman named Weiler, who had slain his brother and for that crime was condemned to wander ceaselessly until it recovered a certain piece of paper hidden in a vault under the cathedral. On hearing this, she solemnly assured it that by prayer alone could its sins be forgiven and pardon obtained, and thereupon she set herself to teach it to pray. Ultimately, with a most joyous countenance, the ghost told her that she had indeed led it to its Redeemer and won its release; and at the same time seven tiny spirits—the spirits of the children it had had on earth—appeared in a circle about it and sang melodiously. Nor did they leave her until the protecting apparition of her grandmother interrupted their thanksgivings and bade them be gone.

Whether or no the happy ghost notified others in kindred plight of the success that had attended her efforts, it is certain that, if the contemporary records are to be accepted, the few short years of life remaining to her were largely occupied in ministering to the wants of distressed spirits. Phantom monks, nobles, peasants, pressed upon her with terrible tales of misdeeds unatoned, and begged her to instruct them in the prayers which were essential to salvation. There was one specially importunate group, the apparitions of a young man, a young woman, and a new-born child wrapped in ghostly rags, which gave her no peace for months. The child, they said, was theirs and had been murdered by them, and the young woman in her turn had been murdered by the young man. Naturally, they were in an unhappy frame of mind, and until she was able to send them on their way rejoicing their conduct and language were so extravagant that they appalled her more than did any other of the numerous seekers for grace and rest.

The dead were not the only ones to whom she ministered. Side by side with the gift of ghost-seeing and ghost-conversing, and with the no less remarkable gift of speaking in an unknown tongue and of setting forth the mysteries of the hereafter, she developed the peculiar faculty of peering into the innermost being of spirits still in the flesh, detecting the obscure causes of disease, and prescribing remedies. Strange to say, her own health remained poor, and gradually she became so feeble that from day to day her death seemed imminent. But her parents were resolved to do all they could for her, and at last bethought themselves of placing her in the hands of the much talked of physician, Justinus Kerner, who lived in the pleasant valley town of Weinsberg and was said to be an adept in every branch of the healing art, notably in the mesmerism which alone appeared to benefit her. To Kerner, therefore, she was sent; and it is not difficult to imagine the delight with which she exchanged the gloomy mountain forests for the verdant meadows and fragrant vineyards of Weinsberg.

Kerner, who is better known to the present generation as mystic and poet than as physician, was justly accounted one of the celebrities of the day. Eccentric and visionary, he was yet a man of solid learning and an intense patriot. It was owing to him, as his biographers fondly recall, that Weinsberg's most glorious monument, the well named Weibertrube, was not suffered to fall into utter neglect, but was instead restored to remind all Germans of that distant day, in the long gone twelfth century, when the women of Weinsberg, securing from the conqueror the promise that their lives would be spared, and that they might take with them from the doomed city their most precious belongings, staggered forth under the burden not of jewels and treasure but of their husbands, whom they carried in their arms or on their backs. Thus was a massacre averted, and thus did the name of "Woman's Faithfulness" attach itself to the castle in the shadow of which Kerner spent his days. But at the time of which we write neither the castle nor poetry held first place in his thoughts; instead, he was absorbed in the practice of his profession. And so, with the ardor of the enthusiast and the sympathy of the true physician, he welcomed to Weinsberg the sufferer of whom he had heard much and of whom he was to become both doctor and biographer.

It was in November, 1826, that he first met her. She was then twenty-five, and thus had been for six years in a state of almost constant ill health. Her very appearance moved him profoundly. Her fragile body, he relates in the graphic word picture he drew, enveloped her spirit but as a gauzy veil. She was extremely small, with Oriental features and dark-lashed eyes that were at once penetrating and "prophetic." When she spoke his conviction deepened that he was looking on one who belonged more to the world of the dead than to the world of the living; and he speedily became persuaded that she actually did, as she claimed, commune with the dead.

Less than a month after her arrival at Weinsberg, and being in the trance condition that was now frequent with her, she announced to him that she had been visited by a ghost, which insisted on showing her a sheet of paper covered with figures and begged her to give it to his wife, who was still alive and would understand its significance and the duty devolving upon her of making restitution to the man he had wronged in life.

Kerner was thunderstruck at recognizing from her description a Weinsberg lawyer who had been dead for some years and was thought to have defrauded a client out of a large sum of money. Eagerly he plied Frederica with questions, among other things asking her to endeavor to locate the paper of which the ghost spoke.

"I see it," said she, dreamily. "It lies in a building which is sixty paces from my bed. In this I see a large and a smaller room. In the latter sits a tall gentleman, who is working at a table. Now he goes out, and now he returns. Beyond these rooms there is one still larger, in which are some chests and a long table. On the table is a wooden thing—I cannot name it—and on this lie three heaps of paper; and in the center one, about the middle of the heap, lies the sheet which so torments him."

Knowing that this was an exact account of the office of the local bailiff, Kerner hastened to that functionary with the astonishing news, and was still more astonished when the bailiff told him that he had been occupied precisely as she said. Together they searched among the papers on the table; but could find none in the lawyer's handwriting. Frederica, however, was insistent, adding that one corner of the paper in question was turned down and that it was enclosed in a stout brown envelope. A second search proved that she was right, and on opening the paper it was found to contain not only figures but an explicit reference to a private account book of which the lawyer's widow had denied all knowledge. Still more striking was the fact, according to Kerner's narrative, that when the bailiff, as a test, placed the paper in a certain position on his desk and went to Frederica, pretending that he had it with him, she correctly informed him where it was and read it off to him word by word.

Although the sequel was rather unsatisfactory, inasmuch as the widow persisted in asserting that she knew nothing of a private account book and refused to yield a penny to the injured client, Kerner was so impressed by this exhibition of supernatural power that, in order to study his patient more closely, he had her removed from her lodgings to his own house. Thither also, as soon as he learned that their presence seemed to increase her susceptibility to the occult influences by which she was surrounded, he brought her sister and the maid servant of the dancing candle episode.

Then ensued greater marvels than had ever bewitched the family at Oberstenfeld. Invisible hands threw articles of furniture at the enthusiastic doctor and his friends; ghostly fingers sprinkled lime and gravel on the flooring of his halls and rooms; spirit knuckles beat lively tattoos on walls, tables, chairs, and bedsteads. And all the while ghosts with criminal pasts flocked in and out, seeking consolation and advice. Only once or twice, however, did the physician himself see anything even remotely resembling a ghost. On one occasion a cloudy shape floated past his window; and on another he saw at Frederica's bedside a pillar of vapor, which she afterward told him was the specter of a tall old man who had visited her twice before.

But if he neither saw the ghosts nor heard them speak, it was sufficiently demonstrated to him that they were really in evidence. The knocking, furniture throwing, and gravel sprinkling were the least of the wonders of which it was permitted him to be a witness. Once, when Frederica was taking an afternoon nap, a spirit that was evidently solicitous for her comfort drew off her boots, and in his presence carried them across the room to where her sister was standing by a window. Again at midnight, after a preliminary knocking on the walls, he observed another spirit, or possibly the same, open a book she had been reading which was lying on her bed.

Most marvelous of all, when her father died she herself enacted the rôle of ghost, the news of his death being conveyed to her supernaturally and her cry of anguish being supernaturally conveyed back to the room where his corpse lay, in

Oberstenfeld, and where it was distinctly heard by the physician who had attended him in his last moments. After this crowning piece of testimony the good Kerner felt that no doubt of her unheard of powers could remain in the most skeptical mind.

Judge, then, of his dismay and grief when he saw her visibly fading away, daily growing more ethereal of form and feature, more weak in body and spirit. It was his belief that the ghosts were robbing her of her vitality, and earnestly but vainly he strove to banish them. She herself declared, with a tone of indescribable relief, that she knew the end was near, and that she welcomed it, as she longed to attain the quiet of the grave with her father and Grandfather and Grandmother Schmidgall. When Kerner sought to cheer her by the assurance that she yet had many years to live, she silenced him with the tale of a gruesome vision. Three times, she said, there had appeared to her at dead of night a female figure, wrapped in black and standing beside an open and empty coffin, to which it beckoned her. But before she died she wished to see again the mountains of her childhood; and to the mountains Kerner carried her. There, on August 5, 1829, peacefully and happily, to the singing of hymns and the sobbing utterance of prayers, her soul took its flight.

But, unlike Kerner, who hastened back to Weinsberg to write the biography of this "delicate flower who lived upon sunbeams," we must shake off the spell of her strange personality and ask seriously what manner of mortal she was. This inquiry is the more imperative since the doings of the tambourine players and automatic writers, of whom so much is made in certain quarters to-day, pale into insignificance beside the story of her remarkable career.

Now, in point of fact, the evidence bearing out the claim that she saw and talked with the dead is practically confined to the account written by the mourning Kerner, whom no one would for a moment call an unprejudiced witness. Already deeply immersed in the study of the marvelous, his mind absorbed in the weird phenomena of the recently discovered science of animal magnetism, she came to him both as a patient and as a living embodiment of the mysteries that held for him a boundless fascination, and once he found reason to believe in her alleged supernormal powers, there was nothing too fantastic or extravagant to which he would not give ready credence and assent.

His lengthy record of "facts" includes not only what he himself saw or thought he saw, but every tale and anecdote related to him by the seeress and her friends, and also includes so many incidents of supernaturalism on the part of others that it would well seem that half the peasant population of Würtemberg were ghost seers. Besides this, detailed as his narrative is, it is lacking in precisely those details which would give it evidential value; so lacking, indeed, that even such a spiritistic advocate as the late F. W. H. Myers pronounced it "quite inadequate" for citation in support of the spiritistic theory.

Nevertheless, taking his extraordinary document for what it is worth, careful consideration of it leads to the conclusion that it contains the story not so much of a great fraud as of a great tragedy. It is obvious that there was frequent and barefaced trickery, particularly on the part of Frederica's sister and the ubiquitous servant girl; but it is equally certain that Frederica herself was a wholly abnormal creature, firmly self-deluded, one might say self-hypnotized, into the belief that the dead consorted with her. And it is hardly less certain that in her singular state of body and mind she gave evidence not indeed of supernatural but of telepathic and clairvoyant powers on which she and those about her, in that unenlightened age, could not but put a supernatural interpretation.

It is not difficult to trace the origin of the nervous and mental disease from which she suffered. Kerner's account of her childhood shows plainly that she was born temperamentally imaginative and unstable and that she was raised in an environment well calculated to exaggerate her imaginativeness and instability. Ghosts and goblins were favorite topics of conversation among the peasantry of Prevorst, while the children with whom she played were many of them unstable like herself, neurotic, hysterical, and the victims of St. Vitus's dance. The weird and uneasy ideas and feelings which thus early took possession of her were given firmer lodgment by her unfortunate sojourn with grave-haunting Grandfather Schmidgall. After this, it seems, she suffered for a year from some eye trouble, and every physician knows how close the connection is between optical disease and hallucinations. Then came a brief period of seeming normality, the lull before the storm which burst in full force with her marriage to a man she did not love. From that time, the helpless victim of hysteria in its most deep-seated and obstinate form, she gave herself unreservedly to the delusions which both arose from and intensified her physical ills—ills which after all had a purely mental basis. "If I doubted the reality of these apparitions," she once told Kerner, "I should be in danger of insanity; for it would make me doubt the reality of everything I saw."

It does not affect this view of the case that she unquestionably coöperated with her conscienceless sister and the servant girl in the production of the fraudulent phenomena to which Kerner testifies. Their cheating was probably done for the sole purpose of making sure of the comfortable berth in which the physician's credulity had placed them. Hers, on the other hand, was the deceit of an irresponsible mind, of one living in such an atmosphere of unreality that she could readily persuade herself that the knockings, candle dancings, book openings, and similar acts were the work not of her own hands but of the ghosts which tormented her. Indeed, researches of recent years in the field of abnormal psychology show it is quite possible that she was absolutely ignorant of any personal participation in the movements and sounds which caused such widespread mystification. Sympathy and pity, therefore, should take the place of condemnation when we follow the course of her eventful and unhappy life.

VIII

THE MYSTERIOUS MR. HOME

"So you've brought the devil to my house, have you?"

"No, no, aunty, no! It's not my fault."

With an angry gesture the woman, tall, large boned, harsh visaged, pushed back her chair and advanced threateningly toward the pale, anemic looking youth of seventeen, who sat cowering at the far end of the breakfast table.

"You know this is your doing. Stop it at once!"

The other gazed helplessly about him, while from every side of the room came a volley of raps and knocks. "It is not my doing," he muttered. "I cannot help it."

"Begone then! Out of my sight!"

Left to herself and to silence,—for with her nephew's departure the noise instantly ceased,—she fell into gloomy meditation. She was an exceedingly ignorant, but a profoundly religious woman. She had heard much of the celebrated Fox sisters, with tales of whose strange actions in the neighboring State of New York the countryside was then ringing, and she recognized, or imagined she recognized, a striking similarity between their performances and the tumult of the last few minutes. It was her firm belief that the Fox girls were victims of demoniac influence, and no less surely did she deem it impossible to attribute the recent disturbance to human agency. Her nephew was not given to practical jokes; there had been nothing unusual in his manner; he had greeted her cheerily as usual, and quietly taken his seat. But with his advent, and she shuddered at the remembrance, the knockings had begun. There could be only one explanation— the boy, however unwittingly, had placed himself in the power of the devil. What to do, however, she knew not, and fumed and fretted the entire morning, until upon his reappearance at noon the knockings broke out again. Then her mind was quickly made up.

"Look you!" said she to him. "We must rid you of the evil that is in you. I will have the ministers reason with you and pray for you, and that at once."

True to her word, she despatched a messenger to the three clergymen of the little Connecticut village in which she made her home, and all three promptly responded to her request. But their visits and their prayers proved fruitless. Indeed, the more they prayed the louder the knocks became; and presently, to their astonishment and dismay, the very furniture appeared bewitched, dancing and leaping as though alive. "Verily," said one to his irate aunt, "the boy is possessed of the devil." To make matters worse, the neighbors, hearing of the weird occurrences, besieged the house day and night, their curiosity whetted by a report that, exactly as in the case of the Fox sisters, communications from the dead were being received through the knockings. Incredible as it seemed, this report found speedy confirmation. Before the week was out the lad told his aunt:

"Last night there came raps to me spelling words, and they brought me a message from the spirit of my mother."

"And what, pray, was the message?"

"My mother's spirit said to me, 'Daniel, fear not, my child. God is with you, and who shall be against you? Seek to do good. Be truthful and truth loving, and you will prosper, my child. Yours is a glorious mission—you will convince the infidel, cure the sick, and console the weeping.'"

"A glorious mission," mocked the aunt, her patience utterly exhausted,—"a glorious mission to bedevil and deceive, to plague and torment! Away, away, and darken my doors no more!"

"Do you mean this, aunty?"

"Mean it, Daniel? Never shall it be said of me that I gave aid and comfort to Satan or child of Satan's. Pack, and be off!"

In this way was Daniel Dunglas Home launched on a career that was to prove one of the most marvelous, if not the most marvelous, in the annals of mystification. But at the time there was no reason to anticipate the remarkable achievements which the future held in store for him. He was fitted for no calling. Ever since his aunt had adopted him in far-away Scotland, where he was born of obscure parentage in 1833, he had led a life of complete dependence, not altogether cheerless but deadening to initiative and handicapping him terribly for the task of making his way in the world. His health was broken, his pockets were empty, he was without friends. Cast upon his own resources under such conditions, it seemed but too probable that failure and an early death would be his portion.

Two things only were in his favor. The first was his native determination and optimism; the second, the interest aroused by published reports of the phenomena that had led to his expulsion from his aunt's house. Already, although only a few days had elapsed since the knockings were first heard, the newspapers had given the story great publicity, and their accounts were greedily devoured by an ever-widening circle of readers, quite willing to regard such happenings as evidence of the intervention of the dead in the affairs of the living. It was, it must be remembered, an era of wide-spread enthusiasm and credulity, the heyday period of spiritism. So soon, therefore, as it became known that young Home was at liberty to go where he would, invitations were showered on him.

Among these was one from the nearby town of Willimantic, and thither Home journeyed in the early spring of 1851. It was determined that an attempt should be made to demonstrate his mediumship by the table tilting process then coming into vogue among spiritists, and the result exceeded all expectations. The table, according to an eye-witness of the first séance, not only moved without physical contact, but on request turned itself upside down, and overcame a spectator's efforts to prevent its motion. True, when this spectator "grasped its leg and held it with all his strength" the table "did not move so freely as before." Still, it moved, and Home's fame mounted apace. From town to town he traveled, holding séances at which, if contemporary accounts are to be believed, he gave exhibitions of supernatural power far and away ahead of all other of the numerous mediums who were by this time springing up throughout the Eastern States. On one occasion, we are told, the spirits communicated through him the whereabouts of missing title deeds to a tract of land then in litigation; on another, they enabled him to prescribe successfully for an invalid for whom no hope was entertained; and time after time they conveyed to those in his séance room messages of more or less vital import, besides vouchsafing to them "physical" phenomena of the greatest variety.

What was most remarkable was the fact that the young medium steadfastly refused to accept payment for his services. "My gift," he would solemnly say, "is free to all, without money and without price. I have a mission to fulfil, and to its fulfilment I will cheerfully give my life." Naturally this attitude of itself made for converts to the spiritistic beliefs of which he was such a successful exponent, and its influence was powerfully reinforced by the result of an investigation conducted in the spring of 1852 by a committee headed by the poet, William Cullen Bryant, and the Harvard professor, David G. Wells. Briefly, these declared in their report that they had attended a séance with Home in a well lighted room, had seen a table move in every direction and with great force, "when we could not perceive any cause of motion," and even "rise clear of the floor and float in the atmosphere for several seconds"; had in vain tried to inhibit its action by sitting on it; had occasionally been made "conscious of the occurrence of a powerful shock, which produced a vibratory motion of the floor of the apartment in which we were seated"; and finally were absolutely certain that they had not been "imposed upon or deceived."

The report, to be sure, did not specify what, if any, means had been taken to guard against fraud, its only reference in this connection being a statement that "Mr. D. D. Home frequently urged us to hold his hands and feet." But it none the less created a tremendous sensation, public attention being focused on the fact that an awkward, callow, country lad had successfully sustained the scrutiny of men of learning, intelligence, and high repute. No longer, it would seem, could there be doubt of the validity of his claims, and greater demands than ever were made on him. As before, he willingly responded, adding to his repertoire, if the term be permissible, new feats of the most startling character. Thus, at a séance in New York a table on which a pencil, two candles, a tumbler, and some papers had been placed, tipped over at an angle of thirty degrees without disturbing in the slightest the position of the movable objects on its surface. Then at the medium's bidding the pencil was dislodged, rolling to the floor, while the rest remained motionless; and afterward the tumbler.

A little later occurred the first of Home's levitations when at the house of a Mr. Cheney in South Manchester, Connecticut, he is said to have been lifted without visible means of support to the ceiling of the séance room. To quote from an eye-witness's narrative: "Suddenly, and without any expectation on the part of the company, Mr. Home was taken up in the air. I had hold of his feet at the time, and I and others felt his feet—they were lifted a foot from the floor.... Again and again he was taken from the floor, and the third time he was carried to the lofty ceiling of the apartment, with which his hand and head came in gentle contact." A far cry, this, from the simple raps and knocks that had ushered in his mediumship.

Now, however, an event occurred that threatened to cut short alike his "mission" and his life. Never of robust health, he fell seriously ill of an affection that developed into tuberculosis. The medical men whom he consulted unanimously declared that his only hope lay in a change of climate, and, taking alarm, his spiritistic friends generously subscribed a large sum to enable him to visit Europe. Incidentally, no doubt, they expected him to serve as a missionary of the new faith, and it may be said at once that in this expectation they were not deceived. No one ever labored more earnestly and successfully in behalf of spiritism than did Daniel Dunglas Home from the moment he set foot on the shores of England in April, 1855; and no one in all the history of spiritism achieved such individual renown, not in England alone but in almost every country of the Continent.

It is from this point that the mystery of his career really becomes conspicuous. Hitherto, with the exception of the Bryant-Wells investigation, which could hardly be called scientific, his pretensions had not been seriously tested, and operating as he did among avowed spiritists he had enjoyed unlimited opportunities for the perpetration of fraud. But henceforth, skeptics as well as believers having ready access to him, he found himself not infrequently in a thoroughly hostile environment, and subjected to the sharpest criticism and most unrestrained abuse. Nevertheless, he was able not simply to maintain but to augment the fame of his youth, and after a mediumship of more than thirty years, could claim the unique distinction of not once having had a charge of trickery proved against him.

Besides this, overcoming with astounding ease the handicaps of his humble birth and lack of education, his life was one continued round of social triumphs of the highest order; for he speedily won and retained to the day of his death the confidence and friendship of leaders of society in every European capital. With them, in castle, château, and mansion, he made his home, always welcome and always trusted; and in his days of greatest stress, days of ill health, vilification, and legal entanglements, they rallied unfailingly to his aid. Add again that Kings and Queens vied with one another in entertaining and rewarding him, and it is possible to gain some idea of the heights scaled by this erstwhile Connecticut country boy.

He began modestly enough by taking rooms at a quiet London hotel, where, his fame having spread through the city, he soon had the pleasure of giving a séance to two such distinguished personages as Lord Brougham and Sir David Brewster. Both retired thoroughly mystified, though the latter some months later asserted that while he "could not account for all" he had witnessed, he had seen enough to satisfy himself "that they could all be produced by hands and feet,"—a statement which, by the way, was at variance from one he had made at the time, and involved him in a most unpleasant controversy. After Brougham and Brewster came a long succession of other notables, including the novelist Sir Bulwer Lytton, to whom a most edifying experience was granted. Rapping away as usual, the table suddenly indicated that it had a message for him, and the alphabet being called over in the customary spiritistic style, it spelled out:

"I am the spirit who influenced you to write Zanoni."

"Indeed!" quoth Lytton, with a skeptical smile. "Suppose you give me a tangible proof of your presence?"

"Put your hand under the table."

No sooner done, than the invisible being gave him a hearty handshake, and proceeded:

"We wish you to believe in the—" It stopped.

"In what? In the medium?"

"No."

At that moment there came a gentle tapping on his knee, and looking down he found on it a small cardboard cross that had been lying on another table. Lytton, the story goes, begged permission to keep the cross as a souvenir, and promised that he would remember the spirit's injunction. For Home, of course, the incident was a splendid advertisement, as were the extravagant reports spread broadcast by other visitors. Consequently, when he visited Italy in the autumn as the guest of one of his English patrons, he gained instant recognition and was enabled to embark with phenomenal ease on his Continental crusade.

In order to reach the most striking manifestations of his peculiar ability, we must pass hurriedly over the events of the next few years, although they are perhaps the most picturesque of his career, including as they do séances with the third Napoleon and his Empress, with the King of Prussia, and with the Emperor of Russia. In Russia he was married to the daughter of a noble Russian family, and for groomsmen at his wedding had Count Alexis Tolstoi, the famous poet, and Count Bobrinski, one of the Emperor's chamberlains. This was in 1858, and shortly afterward he returned to England to repeat his spiritistic triumphs of 1855, and increase the already large group of influential and titled friends whose doors were ever open to him. Had it not been for their generosity, it is difficult, indeed, to see how he could have lived, for his time was almost altogether devoted to the practice of spiritism, and he was never known to accept a fee for a séance. As it was, he lived very well, now the guest of one, now of another, and the frequent recipient of costly presents. From England he fared back to the Continent, again traversing it by leisurely stages. Thus nearly a decade passed before the occurrence of the first of the several phenomena that have won Home an enduring place among the greatest lights of spiritism.

At that time his English patrons included the Viscount Adare and the Master of Lindsay, who have since become respectively the Earl of Dunraven and the Earl of Crawford. They were sitting one evening (December 16, 1868) in an upper room of a house in London with Home and a Captain Wynne, when Home suddenly left the room and entered the adjoining chamber. The opening of a window was then heard, and the next moment, to the amazement of all three, they perceived Home's form floating in the dim moonlight outside the window of the room in which they were seated. For an instant it hovered there, at a height of fully seventy feet above the pavement, and then, smiling and debonnair, Home was with them again. Another marvel immediately followed. At Home's request Lord Dunraven closed the window out of which the medium was supposed to have been carried by the spirits, and on returning observed that the window had not been raised a foot, and he did not see how a man could have squeezed through it. "Come," said Home, "I will show you." Together they went into the next room.

"He told me," Lord Dunraven reported, "to open the window as it was before. I did so. He told me to stand a little distance off; he then went through the open space, head first, quite rapidly, his body being nearly horizontal and apparently rigid. He came in again feet foremost, and we returned to the other room. It was so dark I could not see clearly how he was supported outside. He did not appear to grasp, or rest upon the balustrade, but rather to be swung out and in."

To Lord Dunraven and Lord Crawford again was given the boon of witnessing another of Home's most sensational performances, and on more than one occasion. This may best be described in Lord Crawford's own words, as related in his testimony to the London Dialectical Society's committee which in 1869 undertook an inquiry into the claims of spiritism.

"I saw Mr. Home," declared Lord Crawford, "in a trance elongated eleven inches. I measured him standing up against the wall, and marked the place; not being satisfied with that, I put him in the middle of the room and placed a candle in front of him, so as to throw a shadow on the wall, which I also marked. When he awoke I measured him again in his natural size, both directly and by the shadow, and the results were equal. I can swear that he was not off the ground or standing on tiptoe, as I had full view of his feet, and, moreover, a gentleman present had one of his feet placed over Home's insteps.... I once saw him elongated horizontally on the ground. Lord Adare was present. Home seemed to grow at both ends, and pushed myself and Adare away."

The publication of this evidence and of the details of the mid-air excursion provoked, as may be imagined, a heated discussion, and doubtless had considerable influence in inducing the famous scientist, Sir William Crookes, to engage in the series of experiments which he carried out with Home two years later. This was at once the most searching investigation to which Home was ever subjected, and the most signal triumph of his career. Sir William's proposal was hailed with the greatest satisfaction by the critics of spiritism in general and of Home in particular. Here, it was said, was a man fully qualified to expose the archimpostor who had been so justly pilloried in Browning's "Mr. Sludge the Medium"; here was a scientist, trained to exact knowledge and close observation, who would not be deceived by the artful tricks of a conjurer. It was pleasant too to learn that in order to circumvent any attempts at sleight of hand, Sir William intended using instruments specially designed for test purposes, and which he was confident could not be operated fraudulently.

But Home, or the spirits proved too strong for even Sir William Crookes and his instruments. In Sir William's presence, in fact, there was a multiplication of mysteries. The instruments registered results which seemed inexplicable by any natural law; a lath, cast carelessly on a table, rose in the air, nodded gravely to the astonished scientist, and proceeded to tap out messages alleged to come from the world beyond; chairs moved in ghostly fashion up and down the room; invisible beings lifted Home himself from the floor; spirit hands were seen and felt; an accordeon, held by Sir William, played tunes apparently of its own volition, and afterward floated about the room, still playing. And all this, according to the learned investigator, "in a private room that almost up to the commencement of the séance has been occupied as a living room, and surrounded by private friends of my own, who not only will not countenance the slightest deception, but who are watching narrowly everything that takes place."

In the end, so far from announcing that he had convicted Home of fraud, Sir William published an elaborate account of his séances, and gave it as his solemn belief that with Home's assistance he had succeeded in demonstrating the existence of a hitherto unknown force. This was scarcely what had been expected by the scientific world, which had eagerly awaited his verdict, and loud was the tumult that followed. But Sir William stood manfully by his guns, and Home— bland, inscrutable, mysterious Home—figuratively shrugging his shoulders at denunciations to which he had by this time become perfectly accustomed, added another leaf to his spiritistic crown of laurels, and betook himself anew to his friends on the Continent, where, despite increasing ill health, he continued to prosecute his "mission" for many prosperous years.

As a matter of fact, throughout the period of his mediumship, that is to say, from 1851 to 1886, the year of his death, he experienced only one serious reverse, and this did not involve any exposure of the falsity of his claims. But it was serious enough, in all conscience, and calls for mention both because it emphasizes the contrast between his earlier and his later life, and because it throws a luminous sidelight on the methods by which he achieved his unparalleled success. When he was in London in 1867 he made the acquaintance of an elderly, impressionable English-woman named Lyon, who immediately conceived a warm attachment for him and stated her intention of adopting him as her son. Carrying out this plan, she settled on him the snug little fortune of one hundred and twenty thousand dollars, which she subsequently increased until it amounted to no less than three hundred thousand dollars. Home at the time was a widower, and it was his belief, as he afterward stated in court, that the woman desired him to marry her.

In any event her affection cooled as rapidly as it had begun, and the next thing he knew he was being sued for the recovery of the three hundred thousand dollars. The trial was a celebrated case in English law. Lord Dunraven, Lord Crawford, and other of Home's titled and influential friends hurried to his assistance, and many were the affidavits forthcoming to combat the contentions of Mrs. Lyon, who swore that she had been influenced to adopt Home by communications alleged to come through him from her dead husband. Home himself denied that there were any manifestations whatever relating to Mrs. Lyon, whose story, in fact, was so discredited on cross-examination that the presiding judge, the vice-chancellor, caustically declared that her testimony was quite unworthy of belief. Notwithstanding which, he did not hesitate to give judgment in her favor, on the ground that, however worthless her evidence, it had not been satisfactorily shown that her gifts to Home were "acts of pure volition," the presumption being that no reasonable man or woman would have pursued the course she did unless under the pressure of undue influence by the party to be benefited.

If for "undue influence" we read "hypnotism," we shall have a sufficient, and what seems to me the only satisfactory, explanation of the Lyon episode and of the most baffling of Home's feats, his levitations, elongations, and the like. For the rest, bearing in mind the fate of other dealers in turning tables and dancing chairs, he may fairly be regarded in the light Browning regarded him, that is to say as an exceptionally able conjurer who enjoyed the singular good fortune of never being found out. It must be remembered that not once was there applied to him the test which is now recognized as absolutely indispensable in the investigation of mediums who, like Home, are specialists in the production of "physical" phenomena. This test is the demand that the phenomena in question be produced under conditions doing away with the necessity for constant observation of the medium himself.

Even Sir William Crookes, who appreciated to the full the extreme fallibility of the human eye and the ease with which the most careful observer may be deceived by a clever prestidigitator, failed to apply this test to Home; and by so failing laid himself open on the one hand to deception and on the other to the flood of criticism let loose by his scientific colleagues. Thus, the apparatus used in the experiment on which he seems to have laid greatest stress, is described as follows:

"In another part of the room an apparatus was fitted up for experimenting on the alterations in the weight of a body. It consisted of a mahogany board thirty-six inches long by nine and one-half inches wide and one inch thick. At each end a strip of mahogany one and one-half inches wide was screwed on, forming feet. One end of the board rested on a firm table, whilst the other end was supported by a spring balance hanging from a substantial tripod stand. The balance was fitted with a self-registering index, in such a manner that it would record the maximum weight indicated by the pointer. The apparatus was adjusted so that the mahogany board was horizontal, its foot resting flat on the support. In this position its weight was three pounds, as marked by the pointer of the balance. Before Mr. Home entered the room the apparatus had been arranged in position, and he had not seen the object of some parts explained before sitting down."

Now, to give this "test" evidential value, the disembodied spirit supposed to be acting through Home should have caused the registering index to record a change in weight without necessitating, on the spectators' part, constant scrutiny of the medium's movements. But, in point of fact, a change in weight was recorded only when Home placed his fingers on the mahogany board. It is true, that he placed them on the end furthest from the balance, and the evidence seems sufficient that he did not cause the pointer to move by exerting a downward pressure. But as one critic, Mr. Frank Podmore, has suggested there is no proof that he did not find opportunity to tamper with the pointer itself or with some other part of the apparatus by attaching thereto a looped thread or hair. To quote Mr. Podmore:

"It is by the use of such a thread, I venture to suggest, that the watchful observation of Mr. Crookes and his colleagues was evaded. Given a subdued light and opportunity to move about the room—and from detailed notes of later séances it seems probable that Home could do as he liked in both respects—the loop could be attached without much risk of detection to some part of the apparatus, preferably the hook from which the distal end of the board was suspended, the ends [of the thread] being fastened to some part of Home's dress, e.g., the knees of his trousers, if his feet and hands were under effectual observation."

Moreover, it must not be forgotten that, barring the Crookes investigation, Home's manifestations for the most part occurred in the presence of men and women who, if not spiritists themselves, had implicit confidence in his good faith and could by no stretch of the imagination be called trained investigators. Indeed, it seems safe to say that had present day methods of inquiry been employed, as they are employed by the experts of the Society for Psychical Research, Home, so far at any rate as concerned the great bulk of his phenomena, would quickly have been placed in the same gallery as Madam Blavatsky, Eusapia Paladino, and those other wonder workers whom the society has discredited.

In the matter of the levitations and elongations, however, it is not so easy to raise the cry of sheer fraud. Here the only rational explanation, short of supposing that Home availed himself if not of the aid of "spirits" at least of the aid of some unknown physical force, seems to be, as was said, the exercise of hypnotic power. The accounts given by Lord Dunraven, Lord Crawford, and Sir William Crookes show that he had ample scope for the employment of suggestion as a means of inducing those about him to imagine they had seen things which they actually had not seen. In this connection, it seems to me, considerable significance attaches to the following bit of evidence contributed by Lord Crawford with regard to the London levitation:

"I saw the levitations in Victoria Street when Home floated out of the window. He first went into a trance and walked about uneasily; he then went into the hall. While he was away I heard a voice whisper in my ear 'He will go out of one window and in at another.' I was alarmed and shocked at the idea of so dangerous an experiment. I told the company what I had heard and we then waited for Home's return."

After it is stated that Lord Crawford, not long before, had fancied he beheld an apparition of a man seated in a chair, it is easy to imagine the attitude of credulous expectancy with which he, at all events, would "wait for Home's return" via the open window. And the others were doubtless in the same expectant frame of mind. "Expectancy" and "suggestibility" will, indeed, work marvels. I shall never forget how the truth of this was borne home to me some years ago. A friend of mine—now a physician in Maryland, but at that time a medical student in Toronto—occasionally amused himself by giving table-tipping séances, in which he enacted the rôle of medium. There was no suspicion on his sitters' part that he was a "fraud." One evening he invoked the "spirit" of a little child, who had been dead a couple of years, and proceeded to "spell out" some highly edifying messages. Suddenly the séance was interrupted by a shriek and a lady present, not a relative of the dead child, fell to the floor in a faint. When revived, she declared that while the messages were being delivered she had seen the head of a child appear through the top of the table.

With such an instance before us, it can hardly be deemed surprising that Home should be able to play on the imagination of sitters so sympathetic and receptive as Lords Dunraven and Crawford unquestionably were. To tell the truth, Home's whole career, with its scintillating, melodramatic, and uniformly successful phases is altogether inexplicable unless it be assumed that he possessed the hypnotist's qualities in a superlative degree.

It may well be, however, that in the last analysis he not only deceived others but also deceived himself—that his charlatanry was the work of a man constitutionally incapable of distinguishing between reality and fiction in so far as related to the performance of feats contributing to the success of his "mission." In other words, that he was, like other historic personages whom we have already encountered, a victim of dissociation. There is no gainsaying the fact that he was of a distinctly nervous temperament; and it is equally certain that he chose a vocation, and placed himself in an environment, which would tend to make a dissociated state habitual with him. But this is bringing us to the consideration of a psychological problem which would itself require a volume for adequate discussion. Enough to add that, when all is said, and viewed from whatever angle, Daniel Dunglas Home, was, and remains, a fascinating human riddle.

IX

THE WATSEKA WONDER

When the biography of the late Richard Hodgson is written one of its most interesting chapters will be the story of his investigation into the strange case of Lurancy Vennum. Archinquisitor of the Society for Psychical Research, the Sherlock Holmes of professional detectives of the supernatural, in this instance Hodgson was forced to confess himself beaten and to acknowledge that in his belief the only satisfactory solution of the problem before him was to be had through recourse to the hypothesis that the dead can and do communicate with the living.

As is well known, subsequent inquiries, and notably his experiences with the famous Mrs. Piper, led him to the enthusiastic indorsement of this hypothesis; but at the time of the Vennum affair, with the recollection of his triumphs in Europe and Asia fresh in his mind, he was still a thoroughgoing if open minded skeptic; and to Lurancy Vennum must accordingly be given the credit of having brought him, so to speak, to the turning of the ways. Oddly enough too, scarce an effort has been made to assemble evidence in disproof of his findings in that case and to develop a purely naturalistic explanation of a mystery which his verdict went far to establish in the minds of many as a classic illustration of supernatural action. Yet, while it must be admitted that until recently such a task would have been extremely difficult, it may safely be declared that the phenomena manifested through Lurancy Vennum were not a whit more other-worldly than the phenomena produced by the tricksters whom Hodgson himself so skilfully and mercilessly exposed.

To refresh the reader's memory with regard to the facts in the case, it will be recalled that Lurancy Vennum was a young girl, between thirteen and fourteen years old, the daughter of respectable parents living at Watseka, Illinois, a town about eighty-five miles south of Chicago and boasting at the time a population of perhaps fifteen hundred. On the afternoon of July 11, 1877, while sitting sewing with her mother, she suddenly complained of feeling ill, and immediately afterward fell to the floor unconscious, in which state she remained for five hours. The next day the same thing happened; but now, while still apparently insensible to all about her, she began to talk, affirming that she was in heaven and in the company of numerous spirits, whom she described, naming among others the spirit of her brother who had died when she was only three years old. Her parents, deeply religious people of an orthodox denomination, feared that she had become insane, and their fears were increased when, with the passage of time, her "fits," as they called her trances, became more frequent and of longer duration, lasting from one to eight hours and occurring from three to twelve times a day. Physicians could do nothing for her, and by January, 1878, it was decided that she was beyond all hope of cure and that the proper place for her was an insane asylum.

At this juncture her father was visited by Mr. Asa B. Roff, also a resident of Watseka, but having no more than a casual acquaintanceship with the Vennums. He had become interested in the case, he explained, through hearing reports of the intercourse Lurancy claimed to have with the world of the dead, the possibility of which, being a devout spiritist, he did not in the slightest doubt. Moreover, he himself had had a daughter, Mary, long dead, who had been subject to conditions exactly like Lurancy's and had given incontrovertible evidence of possessing supernatural powers of a clairvoyant nature. In her time she too had been deemed insane, but Mr. Roff was confident that she had really been of entirely sound mind, and equally confident that the present victim of "spirit infestation," to use the singular term employed by a later spiritistic eulogist of Lurancy, was also of sound mind. He therefore begged Mr. Vennum not to immure his daughter in an asylum; and Mrs. Roff adding her entreaties, it was finally resolved as a last resort to call in a physician from Janesville, Wisconsin, who was himself a spiritist and would, the Roffs felt sure, be able to treat the case with great success.

This physician, Dr. E. Winchester Stevens, paid his first visit to Lurancy in Mr. Roff's company on the afternoon of January 31. He found the girl, as he afterward related, sitting "near a stove, in a common chair, her elbows on her knees, her hands under her chin, feet curled up on the chair, eyes staring, looking every way like an old hag." She was evidently in an ugly mood, for she refused even to shake hands, called her father "Old Black Dick" and her mother "Old Granny," and at first kept an obstinate silence. But presently, brightening up, she announced that she had discovered that Dr. Stevens was a "spiritual" doctor and could help her, and that she was ready to answer any questions he might put. Now followed a strange dialogue. In reply to his queries she said that her name was not Lurancy Vennum but Katrina Hogan, that she was sixty-three years old, and had come from Germany "through the air" three days before. Changing her manner quickly, she confessed that she had lied and was in reality a boy, Willie Canning, who had died and "now is here because he wants to be." More than an hour passed in this "insane talk," as her weeping parents accounted it, and then, flinging up her hands, she fell headlong in a state of cataleptic rigidity.

Dr. Stevens promptly renewed his questioning, at the same time taking both her hands in his and endeavoring to "magnetize" her, to quote his own expression. It soon developed, according to the replies she made, that she was no longer on earth but in heaven and surrounded by spirits of a far more beneficent character than the so-called Katrina and Willie. With all the earnestness of an ardent spiritist, the doctor immediately suggested that she allow herself to be controlled by a spirit who would prevent those that were evil and insane from returning to trouble her and her family, and would assist her to regain health. To which she answered that she would gladly do so, and that among the spirits around her was one that the angels strongly recommended for this very purpose.

It was, she said, the spirit of a young girl who on earth had been named Mary Roff.

"Why," cried Mr. Roff, "that is my daughter, who has been in heaven these twelve years. Yes, let her come. We'll be glad to have her come."

Come she did, as the greatly bewildered Mr. Vennum testified next morning during a hasty visit to Mr. Roff's office.

"My girl," said he, "had a sound night's sleep after you and Dr. Stevens left us; but to-day she asserts that she is Mary Roff, refuses to recognize her mother or myself, and demands to be taken to your house."

At this amazing information, Mrs. Roff and her surviving daughter Minerva, who since Mary's death had married a Mr. Alter, promptly went to see Lurancy. From a seat at the window she beheld them approaching down the street, and with an exultant cry exclaimed, "Here comes my ma, and 'Nervie'!" the name by which Mary Roff had been accustomed to call her sister in girlhood. Running to the door and throwing her arms about them as they entered, she hugged and kissed them with expressions of endearment and with whispering allusions to past events of which she as Lurancy could in their opinion have had absolutely no knowledge.

Mr. Roff who came afterward, she greeted in the same affectionate way, while treating the members of her own family as though they were entire strangers. To her father and mother it seemed that this must be only a new phase of her insanity, but to the Roffs there remained no doubt that in her they beheld an actual reincarnation of the girl whom they had buried twelve years before—that is to say, when Lurancy herself was a puny, wailing infant. Eagerly they seconded her entreaties to be allowed to return with them; and, Mrs. Vennum being completely prostrated by this unexpected development, it was soon decided that the little girl should for the time being take up her residence under the Roff roof.

She removed there February 11, and on the way an event occurred that vastly strengthened belief in the reality of her claims. The Vennums and the Roffs lived at opposite ends of Watseka; but the latter family, at the time of Mary's death in 1865, had been occupying a dwelling in a central section of the town. Arrived at this house, Lurancy unhesitatingly turned to enter it, and seemed much astonished when told that her home was elsewhere. "Why," said she, in a positive tone, "I know that I live here." It was indeed with some difficulty that she was persuaded to continue her journey; but once at its end all signs of disappointment vanished and she passed gaily from room to room, identifying objects which she had never seen before but which had been well-known to Mary Roff. Her pseudo-parents were in ecstacies of joy. "Truly," they said to each other, "our daughter who was dead has been restored to us," and anxiously they inquired of her how long they might hope to have her with them. "The angels," was her response, "will let me stay till some time in May—and oh how happy I am!"

Happy and contented she proved herself and, which was remarked by all who saw her, entirely free from the maladies that had so sorely beset both the living

Lurancy and the dead Mary. For her life as Lurancy she appeared to have no remembrance; but she readily and unfailingly recollected everything connected with the career of Mary. She was well aware also that she was masquerading, as it were, in a borrowed body. "Do you remember," Dr. Stevens asked her one day, "the time that you cut your arm?" "Yes, indeed. And," slipping up her sleeve, "I can show you the scar. It was—" She paused, and quickly added, "Oh, this is not the arm; that one is in the ground," and proceeded to describe the spot where Mary had been buried and the circumstances attending her funeral. Old acquaintances of Mary's were greeted as though they had been seen only the day before, although in one or two cases there was lack of recognition, due, it was inferred, to physical changes in the visitor's appearance since Mary had known her on earth.

Tests, suggested and carried out by Dr. Stevens and Mr. Roff, only reinforced the view that they were really dealing with a visitant from the unseen world. For instance, while the little girl was playing outdoors one afternoon, Mr. Roff suggested to his wife that she bring down-stairs a velvet hat that their daughter had worn the last year of her life, place it on the hat stand, and see if Lurancy would recognize it. This was done, and the recognition was instant. With a smile of delight Lurancy picked up the hat, mentioned an incident connected with it, and asked, "Have you my box of letters also?" The box was found, and rummaging through it the child presently cried, "Oh, ma, here is a collar I tatted! Ma, why did you not show me my letters and things before?" One by one she picked out and identified relics dating back to Mary's girlhood, long before Lurancy Vennum had come into the world.

She displayed, too, not a little of the clairvoyant ability ascribed to Mary. The story is told that on one occasion she affirmed that her supposed brother, Frank Roff, would be taken seriously ill during the night; and when, about two o'clock in the morning, he was actually stricken with what is vaguely said to have been "something like a spasm and congestive chill," she directed Mr. Roff to hurry next door where he would find Dr. Stevens.

"But," protested Mr. Roff, "Dr. Stevens is in quite another part of the city to-night."

"No," she calmly said, "he has come back, and you will find him where I say."

Quite incredulous, Mr. Roff gave his neighbor's door-bell a lusty pull, and the next moment was talking to the doctor, who, unknown to the Roffs, was spending the night there. With his aid, it is perhaps worth adding, brother Frank was soon relieved of the "spasm and congestive chill."

In this way, continually surprising but constantly delighting the happy Roffs, Lurancy Vennum remained with them for more than three months, professing complete ignorance of her identity and enacting with the greatest fidelity the rôle of the spirit who was supposed to have taken possession of her. Early in May, however, she called Mrs. Roff to one side and informed her in a voice broken by sobs that Lurancy was "coming back" and that they would soon have to take another farewell of their Mary. This said, a change became apparent in her. She glared wildly around, and in an agitated tone demanded, "Where am I? I was never here before. I want to go home." Mrs. Roff, heartbroken, explained that she had been under the control of Mary's spirit for the purpose of "curing her body," and told her that her parents would be sent for. But within five minutes she had again lost all knowledge of her true identity, and seemingly was Mary Roff once more, overjoyed that she had been permitted to return.

For some days she continued in this state, with only occasional lapses into her original self; then, on the morning of May 21, she announced that the time for definite leave-taking had at last arrived, and with evident grief went about among the neighbors bidding them good-by. It was arranged that "sister Nervie" should take her to Mr. Roff's office, and that Mr. Roff should thence escort her home. En route there were sharp interchanges of personality, with the spirit control dominant; but when the office was reached it became evident that she had fully come into her own again. The night before she had wept bitterly at the thought of leaving her "father." Now she addressed him calmly as "Mr. Roff," called herself Lurancy, and said that her one wish was to see her parents as soon as possible. Nor, as the Vennums were quickly to discover, did she return to torment and alarm them by the weird actions of the preceding months. On the contrary, they found her healthy and normal in mind and body, completely cured, as a result, the Roffs emphatically declared, of the intervention of the spirit of their beloved daughter.

Needless to say, the people of Watseka and the surrounding country had watched with breathless interest the progress of this curious affair; but it was not until three months after the "possession" had ended that the public at large obtained any knowledge of it. The first intimation, outside of unnoticed reports in local newspapers, came through the medium of two articles contributed by Dr. Stevens to the August 3 and 10, 1878, issues of *The Religio-Philosophical Journal,* one of the leading spiritist organs of the United States. Traversing the case in the fullest detail, and emphasizing the fact that up to the moment of writing the principal actor had had no return of the ills from which she had previously suffered, Dr. Stevens gave it as his unqualified conviction that the spirit of Mary Roff had actually revisited earth in the person of Lurancy Vennum, and had been the instrument of her cure. This view naturally commended itself to spiritists, but by the unbelieving it was vigorously combatted, not a few insinuating or openly alleging that Dr. Stevens's narrative was a work of fiction. The veracity of the Roffs was also attacked. "Can the truthfulness of the narrative," one skeptical inquirer wrote Mr. Roff, "be substantiated outside of yourself and those immediately interested? Can it be shown that there was no collusion between the parties?" And another asked him, "Is it a fact, or is it a story made up to see how cunning a tale one can tell?"

Waxing indignant, Mr. Roff wrote a long letter to *The Religio-Philosophical Journal* denouncing the imputation of fraud, giving the names of a number of men who would vouch for his integrity, and concluding with the statement: "I am now sixty years old; have resided in Iroquois county thirty years; and would not now sacrifice what reputation I may have by being party to the publication of such a narrative, if it was not perfectly true."

Following this there appeared in *The Religio-Philosophical Journal* several letters from well-known Illinois professional men warmly indorsing Mr. Roff's character, and an announcement to the effect that the editor, Colonel J. C. Bundy, himself of undoubted honesty, "has entire confidence in the truthfulness of the narrative and believes from his knowledge of the witnesses that the account is unimpeachable in every particular." As for Dr. Stevens, Colonel Bundy declared that he had been personally acquainted with the physician for years, and had "implicit confidence in his veracity." After all this, accusations of perjury and deception were obviously futile, and, no adequate non-spiritistic interpretation being forthcoming, there was an increasing tendency to accept the view advanced by those who had participated in the affair.

Such was the situation at the time of Richard Hodgson's advent. Primarily, as will be remembered by all who have followed the work of the Society for Psychical Research, Dr. Hodgson had come to this country to investigate the trance mediumship of Mrs. Leonora Piper. But his attention having been called to the Vennum mystery, he visited Watseka in April, 1890, and instituted a rigorous cross-examination of the surviving witnesses. Dr. Stevens was dead, and Lurancy herself had married and moved with her husband to Kansas, but Dr. Hodgson was able to interview Mr. and Mrs. Roff, Mrs. Alter, and half a dozen neighbors who had personal knowledge of the "possession." All answered his questions freely and fully, reiterating the facts as given in Dr. Stevens's narrative, and adding some interesting information hitherto not made public. In the main this bore on the question of identity and tended to vindicate the reincarnation theory. It also developed that while Lurancy had grown to be a strong, healthy woman, she had had occasional returns of Mary's spirit in the years immediately following the chief visitation; but that these had ceased with her marriage to a man who, Roff regretfully observed, had never made himself acquainted with spiritism and therefore "furnished poor conditions for further development in that direction."

Appreciating the fact that Mr. Roff and his family would furnish the best possible conditions for such development, and that he must be on his guard against unconscious exaggeration and misstatement, Dr. Hodgson nevertheless deemed the evidence presented to him too strong to be explained away on naturalistic grounds. Contributing to *The Religio-Philosophical Journal* an account of his inquiry and of the additional data it had brought to light, he described the case as "unique among the records of supernormal occurrences," and frankly admitted that he could not "find any satisfactory interpretation of it except the spiritistic."

Yet, as was said at the outset, it may now be affirmed that another interpretation is possible, and one far more satisfactory than the spiritistic; this, too, without impeaching in any way the truthfulness of the testimony given by Dr. Stevens, the Roffs, and the numerous other witnesses. To begin: apart from the supernatural implications forced into it by the appearance of the so-called spirit control, it is clear that the affair bears a striking resemblance to the instances of "secondary" or "multiple" personality which recent research has discovered in such numbers, and which are due to perfectly natural, if often obscure, causes. In these, it has already been pointed out, as the result of an illness, a blow, a shock, or some other unusual stimulus, there is a partial or complete effacement of the original personality of the victim and its replacement by a new personality, sometimes of radically different characteristics from the normal self.

A sufficient example is the case of the Rev. Thomas C. Hanna, for knowledge of which the scientific world is indebted to Dr. Boris Sidis. Following a fall from his carriage, Mr. Hanna, a Connecticut clergyman, lost all consciousness of his identity, had no memory for the events of his life prior to the accident, recognized none of his friends, could not read or write, nor so much as walk or talk,—was, in fact, like a child new born. On the other hand, as soon as the rudiments of education were acquired by him once more, he showed himself the possessor of a vigorous, independent, self-reliant personality, lacking all knowledge of the original personality, but still able to adapt himself readily to his environment and make headway in the world. Ultimately, through methods which are distinctively modern, Dr. Sidis was able to recall the vanished self, and, fusing the secondary self with it, restore the clergyman to his former sphere of usefulness.

This, of course, is an extreme example. The usual procedure is for the secondary personality to retain some of the characteristics of the original self—as the ability to read, write, etc.—and give itself a name. In this way Ansel Bourne, the Rhode Island itinerant preacher, became metamorphosed into A. J. Brown, and, without any recollection of his former career or relationships, drifted to Pennsylvania and began an entirely new existence as a shopkeeper in a small country town. Similarly with Dr. R. Osgood Mason's patient, Alma Z., in whom the secondary personality assumed the odd name of "Twoey," spoke, as Dr. Mason phrased it, "in a peculiar child-like and Indianlike dialect," and announced that her mission was to cure the broken down physical organism of the original self, which remained completely in abeyance so long as "Twoey" was in evidence. Here, as is apparent, we have a case almost identical with that of Lurancy Vennum, the sole difference being that "Twoey"—who, by the way, is credited with having exercised seemingly supernormal powers—did not pose as a returned visitant from the world of spirits.

Thus far, then, depending on the argument from analogy, the presumption is strong that Lurancy's case belongs to the same category as the cases just mentioned. In the one, as in the others, we have loss of the original self, development of a new self, and the enactment by the latter of a rôle conspicuously alien from that played by the former. The one difficulty in the way of unreserved acceptance of this view is the character of the secondary personality which replaced Lurancy's original personality. Here the positive claim was made that the secondary personality was in reality the personality of a girl long dead, and by way of proof vivid knowledge of the life, circumstances, and conduct of that girl was offered. But on this point considerable light is shed by the discovery that in a number of instances of secondary personality in which no supernatural pretensions are advanced there is a notable sharpening of the faculties, knowledge being obtained telepathically or clairvoyantly; and by the further discovery that it is quite possible to create experimentally secondary selves assuming the characteristics of real persons who have died.

In this the creative force is nothing more or less than suggestion. There is on record, indeed, an instance of mediumship in which the medium, an amateur investigator of the phenomena of spiritism, clearly recognized that his various impersonations were suggested to him by the spectators. This gentleman, Mr. Charles H. Tout, of Vancouver, records that after attending a few séances with some friends he felt a strong impulse to turn medium himself, and assume a foreign personality. Yielding to the impulse, he discovered, much to his amazement, that without losing complete control of his consciousness, he could develop a secondary self that would impose on the beholders as a discarnate spirit. On one occasion he thus acted in a semi-conscious way the part of a dead woman, the mother of a friend present, and the impersonation was accepted as a genuine case of spirit control. On another, having given several successful impersonations, he suddenly felt weak and ill, and almost fell to the floor.

At this point, he stated, one of the sitters "made the remark, which I remember to have overheard, 'It is father controlling him,' and I then seemed to realize who I was and whom I was seeking. I began to be distressed in my lungs, and should have fallen if they had not held me by the hands and let me back gently upon the floor.... I was in a measure still conscious of my actions, though not of my surroundings, and I have a clear memory of seeing myself in the character of my dying father lying in the bed and in the room in which he died. It was a most curious sensation. I saw his shrunken hands and face, and lived again through his dying moments; only now I was both myself, in an indistinct sort of way, and my father, with his feelings and appearance."

All of this Tout explained correctly as "the dramatic working out, by some half conscious stratum of his personality, of suggestions made at the time by other members of the circle, or received in prior experiences of the kind." In most instances, however, the original self is completely effaced, and no consciousness is retained of the performances of the secondary self; but that an avenue of sense is still open is sufficiently demonstrated by the readiness with which, in hypnotic experiments, seemingly insensible subjects respond to the suggestions of the operator. Here, therefore, we find our clue to the solution of the mystery of Lurancy Vennum. A victim of a psychic catastrophe, the cause of which must be left to conjecture in the absence of knowledge of her previous history, she was placed in precisely the position of the adventurous Mr. Tout and of the inert subjects of the hypnotist's art. That is to say, having lost momentarily all knowledge and control of her own personality, the character her new personality would assume depended on the suggestions received from those about her.

Yet not altogether. Dr. Stevens's detailed record contains a reference which indicates strongly that the spiritistic tendency manifest from the onset of her trouble was to some extent predetermined. A few days before the first attack she informed the family that "there were persons in my room last night, and they called 'Rancy, Rancy!' and I felt their breath on my face"; and the next night, repeating the same story, she sought refuge in her mother's bed. These fanciful notions, symptomatic of the coming trouble and possibly provocative of it, would act in the way of a powerful autosuggestion, and would of themselves explain why there resulted an inchoate, tentative, vague personality, instead of the robust, definite personality that assumes control in most cases.

At first, the reader will remember, she sought vainly and wildly and wholly subconsciously—it cannot be made too clear that she was no longer consciously responsible for her acts—for a satisfactory self of ghostly origin. The aged Katrina, the masculine Willie, and other imaginary beings were tried and rejected; principally, no doubt, because her thirteen-year-old imagination was unequal to the task of investing them with satisfactory attributes. From her relatives she obtained no assistance in the strange quest. They, disbelieving in "spirits," persisted in calling her insane—a comfortless and far from beneficial suggestion. But with the intervention of the Roffs and Dr. Stevens everything changed. Not questioning the truth of her assertions, they confirmed her in them, and offered her into the bargain a ready-made personality.

Here at last was something tangible, a starting-point, a foundation-stone. Mary Roff had had a real existence, had had thoughts, feelings, desires, a life of flesh and blood. And Mary, they assured the poor, perturbed, disintegrated self, could help her regain all that she had lost. Very well, let Mary come, and the sooner she came the better. For knowledge of Mary, of her characteristics, her relationships, her friends, her earthly career, it was necessary only to tap telepathically the reservoir of information possessed by Mary's family; and there would be available besides a wealth of data in chance remarks, unconscious hints, unnoticed promptings. She had been too long in search of a personality not to grasp at the opening now afforded. Focused thus by suggestion,—that subtle, all-pervasive influence which man is only now beginning to appreciate,—the basic delusional idea promptly took root, blossomed, and burst into an amazing fruition. Banished were the spurious Katrinas and Willies. In their stead reigned Mary, no less spurious in point of fact, but so cunningly counterfeiting the true Mary that the deception was not once detected.

Mark too how suggestion sufficed not only to create the Mary personality but to expel it and restore the hapless Lurancy to perfect health. If the responsibility for the creation rests on Dr. Stevens and the Roffs, to them likewise belongs the credit for the cure. Their insistence on the fact that Mary's spirit could and would be of assistance, was itself as powerful a suggestion as could be hit upon by the most expert of modern practitioners of psychotherapeutics; and in unconsciously persuading the spirit to set a limit to its time of "possession" they made another suggestion of rare curative value. To the suggestionally inspired fixed idea that she was not Lurancy Vennum but Mary Roff was thus added the fixed idea, derived from the same source, that in May she would become Lurancy Vennum again, and a perfectly well Lurancy. It was as though the Roffs had actually hypnotized her and given her commands that were to be obeyed with the fidelity characteristic of the obedience hypnotized subjects render to the operator.

When the time came the transformation was duly effected, though, as has been seen, not without a struggle, a period of alternating personality, with Mary at one moment supreme and Lurancy at another. But this is a phenomenon that need give us no concern. Exactly the same thing happened in the last stages of the Hanna case. Nor do the fugitive recurrences of the Mary personality signify aught than that Lurancy was still unduly suggestionable. Note that these recurrences, according to the available evidence, developed only when the Roffs paid her visits; and that they ceased entirely upon her marriage to a man not interested in spiritism, and her removal to a distant part of the country.

X

A MEDIEVAL GHOST HUNTER

The name of Dr. John Dee is scarcely known to-day, yet Dr. Dee has some exceedingly well-defined claims to remembrance. He was one of the foremost scientists of the Tudor period in English history. He was famed as a mathematician, astronomer, and philosopher not only in his native land but in every European center of learning. Before he was twenty he penned a remarkable treatise on logic, and he left behind him at his death a total of nearly a hundred works on all manner of recondite subjects. He was the means of introducing into England a number of astronomical instruments hitherto unused, and even unknown, in that country. His lectures on geometry were the delight of all who heard them. In Elizabeth's reign he was frequently consulted by the highest ministers of the crown with regard to affairs of State, and was the confidant of the queen herself, who more than once employed him on secret missions. He was interested in everyday affairs as well as in questions of theoretical importance. The reformation of the calendar long engaged his attention. He charted for Elizabeth her distant colonial dominions. He preached the doctrine of sea-power, and, like Hakluyt, advocated the upbuilding of a strong navy. He was, in some sort, a participant in Sir Humphrey Gilbert's scheme for New World colonization.

In a word, Dr. John Dee was a phenomenally many-sided man in an age that was peculiarly productive of many-sided men. Even yet, the catalogue of his interests and accomplishments is by no means exhausted. Indeed, his chief claim to fame—and, paradoxically enough, the great reason why his reputation practically died with him—lies in the fact that he was one of the earliest of psychical researchers. At a time when all men unhesitatingly entertained a belief in the overshadowing presence of spirits and their constant intervention in human affairs, Dr. Dee resolved to prove, if possible, the actual existence of these mysterious and unseen beings. To encourage him in his ghost-hunting zeal was the hope that the spirits, if actually located by him, might reward his enterprise by unfolding a secret that had long been the despair of all medieval scientists—the secret of the philosopher's stone, of the precious formula whereby the baser metals could be transmuted into shining gold. With the heartiest enthusiasm, therefore, Dr. Dee went to work, and although the spirits with whom he ultimately came into constant communication brought him no gold but many tribulations, he remained an ardent psychical researcher to the day of his death.

Just when he began his explorations of the invisible world it is impossible to say. But it must have been at a very early age, for he was barely twenty-five when a rumor spread that he was dabbling in the black arts. Two years later, in 1554, he was definitely accused of trying to take the life of Queen Mary by enchantments, and on this charge was thrown into prison. For cellmate he had Barthlet Green, who parted from him only to meet an agonizing death in the flames, as an arch-heretic. Dee himself was threatened with the stake, and was actually placed on trial for his life before the dread Court of the Star Chamber. But he seems to have had, throughout his entire career, a singularly plausible manner, and a magnetic, winning personality. He succeeded in convincing his judges both of his innocence of traitorous designs and his religious orthodoxy, and was allowed to go scot free. Elizabeth, on her accession to the throne, naturally looked on him with favor, as one who had been persecuted by her sister; and with the more favor since it was widely reported that he was on the eve of making the grand discovery for which other alchemists had ever labored in vain. A man who might some day make gold at will was certainly not to be despised; rather, he should be cultivated. Nor was her esteem for Dee lessened by the success with which, by astrological calculations, he named a favorable day for her coronation; and, a little later, by solemn disenchantment warded off the ill effects of the Lincoln's Inn Fields incident, when a puppet of wax, representing Elizabeth, was found lying on the ground with a huge pin stuck through its breast.

As a matter of fact, however, Dee was making headway neither in his quest for the philosopher's stone nor in his efforts to prove the existence of a spiritual world. In vain he pored over every work of occultism upon which he could lay his hands, and tried all known means of incantation. Year after year passed without result, until at last he hit on the expedient of crystal-gazing. As every student of things psychical is aware, if one takes a crystal, or glass of water, or other body with a reflecting surface, and gaze at it steadily, he may possibly perceive, after a greater or less length of time, shadowy images of persons or scenes in the substance that fixes his attention. It was so with Dr. Dee, and not having any understanding of the laws of subconscious mental action he soon came to the conclusion that the shadowy figures he saw in the crystal were veritable spirits. From this it was an easy step to imagine that they really talked to him and sought to convey to him a knowledge of the great secrets of this world and the next.

The only difficulty was that he could not understand what they said—or, rather, what he fancied they said. The obvious thing to do was to find a crystal-gazer with the gift of the spirit language, and induce him to interpret for Dr. Dee's benefit the revelations of the images in the glass. Such a crystal-gazer was ready at hand in the person of a young man named Edward Kelley. Among the common people, as Dee well knew, Kelley had the reputation of being a bold and wicked wizard. He had been born in Worcester, and trained in the apothecary's business, but, tempted by the prospect of securing great wealth at a minimum of trouble, he had turned alchemist and magician. It was rumored that on at least one occasion he had disinterred a freshly buried corpse, and by his incantations had compelled the spirit of the dead man to speak to him. There was more truth in the report that the reason he always wore a close-fitting skull-cap was to conceal the loss of his ears, which had been forfeited to the Government of England on his conviction for forgery. Of this last unpleasant incident Dr. Dee seems to have known nothing. At any rate, with child-like confidence, he sent for Kelley, told him of the properties of his magic crystal—which the now thoroughly infatuated doctor represented as having been bestowed on him by the angel Uriel—and asked Kelley if he would interpret for him the wonderful words of the spirits.

Kelley, as shrewd and unscrupulous a man as any in the annals of imposture, readily consented, but on pretty hard terms. He was to be taken in as a member of Dr. Dee's family, retained on a contract, and paid an annual stipend of fifty pounds, quite a large sum in those times. On this understanding he went to work, and day after day, for years, regaled the credulous Dee with monologues purporting to be delivered by the spirits in the crystal. Everything Kelley told him, Dr. Dee faithfully noted down, and many years later, long after both Dee and Kelley had been carried to their graves, these manuscript notes of the séances were published. The volume containing them—a massive, closely printed folio entitled "A True and Faithful Relation of What Passed for Many Years Between Dr. John Dee and Some Spirits"—is one of the great curiosities of literature. A copy of the original edition is before me as I write, and I will quote from it just enough to show the character of the "revelations" vouchsafed to Dee through the mediumship of the cunning Kelley.

"Wednesday, 19 Junii, I made a prayer to God and there appeared one, having two garments in his hands, who answered, 'A good praise, with a wavering mind.'

"God made my mind stable, and to be seasoned with the intellectual leaven, free of all sensible mutability.

"E. K. [said] 'One of these two garments is pure white: the other is speckled of divers colors; he layeth them down before him, he layeth also a speckled cap down before him at his feet; he hath no cap on his head: his hair is long and yellow, but his face cannot be seen.... Now he putteth on his pied coat and his pied cap, he casteth one side of his gown over his shoulder and he danceth, and saith, "There is a God, let us be merry!"'

"E. K. 'He danceth still.'

"'There is a heaven, let us be merry.'

"'Doth this doctrine teach you to know God, or to be skilful in the heavens?'

"'Note it.'

"E. K. 'Now he putteth off his clothes again: now he kneeleth down, and washeth his head and his neck and his face, and shaketh his clothes, and plucketh off the uttermost sole of his shoes, and falleth prostrate on the ground, and saith, "Vouchsafe, oh God, to take away the weariness of my body and to cleanse the filthiness of this dust, that I may be apt for this pureness."'

"E. K. 'Now he taketh the white garment, and putteth it on him.... Now he sitteth down on the desk-top and looketh toward me.... He seemeth now to be turned to a woman, and the very same which we call Galvah.'"

Side by side with the esoteric and transcendental utterances which Kelley credited to the spirits, he cleverly introduced sufficient in the way of references to the elixir of life and the transmutation of metals, to keep alive in Dee's breast the hope of ultimately solving the crucial problems of medieval science. All the money Dee could procure was spent on ingredients for magical formulas, and to such lengths did his enthusiasm carry him that before long he was reduced to poverty. He became so poor, in fact, that when, in the summer of 1583, the Earl of Leicester announced his intention of bringing a notable foreign visitor, Count Albert Lasky of Bohemia, to dine with Dee, the unhappy doctor was compelled to send word that he could not provide a proper dinner. Leicester, moved to pity, reported his plight to the queen, who at once belied her reputation for niggardliness by bestowing a liberal gift on the Sage of Mortlake, as Dee was now styled at the Court. The dinner accordingly took place, and was a tremendous success in more ways than one.

Lasky turned out to be an exceedingly excitable and impressionable man, and his curiosity was so aroused by the occult discourse of his host that he begged to be admitted to the séances. Always alert to the main chance, Kelley, after a few preliminary sittings of unusual picturesqueness, inspired the spirits to predict that Lasky would one day be elected King of Poland. It needed nothing more to induce the happy and hopeful count to invite both Dee and Kelley to return with him to Bohemia. He would, he promised, protect and provide for them; they should live with him in his many turreted castle, and want for nothing. Here, indeed, was a pleasant way out of their present poverty, and Dee and Kelley readily gave consent. Nor did they leave England a moment too soon. Scarcely had they taken ship before a mob, roused to fury by superstitious fears, broke into the philosopher's house at Mortlake and destroyed almost everything that they did not steal—furniture, books, manuscripts, and costly scientific apparatus.

Of this, though, Dee for the moment happily knew nothing. Nor, for all his long intercourse with the spirits, was he able to foresee that he was now embarking on a career of tragic adventure that falls to the lot of few scientists. At first, however, all went well enough. Lasky entertained his learned guests in lavish fashion, and, assuming their garb of long, flowing gown, joined heartily with them in the ceremonies of the séance room. But as time passed and their incantations redounded in no way to his advantage, he gradually lost patience, and broadly hinted that they might better transfer their services to another patron. Whereupon, closely followed by the irrepressible Kelley, Dee removed to the court of the emperor, Rudolph II, at Prague. He had dedicated one of his scientific treatises to the emperor's father, and in his simplicity firmly believed that this would insure him a warm and lasting welcome. But Rudolph, from the outset, showed himself far from well-disposed to Dee, Kelley, and their attendant retinue of invisible spirits. When Dee grandiloquently introduced himself, in a Latin oration, as a messenger from the unseen world, the emperor curtly checked him with the remark that he did not understand Latin. And the next day a hint was given him that, at the request of the papal nuncio, he and Kelley were to be arrested and sent to Rome for trial as necromancers. Before night-fall they were in full flight, to remain homeless wanderers until another Bohemian count, hearing of their presence in his dominions, took them under his protection on the proviso that they were to replenish his exchequer by converting humble pewter into silver and gold.

In this, of course, they signally failed, and the next few years of their lives were years of the greatest misery. This, at any rate, so far as Dee was concerned. Kelley, with pitiless insistence, drew his pay regularly, and when funds were not forthcoming, refused to act as crystal-gazer and spirit interpreter. On one of these occasions Dee tried to replace him by training his son, Arthur Dee, as a crystal-gazer; but, try as he might, the boy said he could see in the crystal nothing but meaningless clouds and specks. Had Dee not been thoroughly infatuated this might have disillusioned him, and convinced him that Kelley had simply been preying on his credulity. But the old man—he was now well advanced in years—saw in his son's failure only proof of Kelley's superior gifts, and by dint of great sacrifices contrived to find the money necessary to persuade him to return to his post. At last a day came when money could no longer be found, and then Kelley definitely determined to break the partnership. According to one account, he informed Dee that, for the sake of his immortal soul, he could no longer have dealings with the spirits; that they were spirits not of good but of evil, and Mephistopheles was their master; and that, did he continue to traffic with them, Mephistopheles would soon have him, body and soul. Another version—given by the astrologer, William Lilly, who is said to have been consulted by the friends of King Charles I. as to the best time for that unhappy monarch to attempt to escape from prison—says that one fine morning Kelley took French leave of Dee, running away with an alchemically inclined friar who had promised him a good income. Whatever the facts of his final rupture with his long-suffering master, it is certain that, after a romantic career, in which he gained a German baronetcy, Kelley was clapped into prison on a charge of fraud, and broke his neck while trying to escape.

Dr. Dee, in the meantime, a sadder if not a really wiser man, had found his way back to England, where he essayed the difficult task of retrieving his ruined fortunes. Elizabeth smiled on him as graciously as ever, and at Christmas time sent to him a royal gift of two hundred angels in gold. But he needed more than an occasional bounty; he needed the assurance of a steady income, and the chance to pursue again his scientific studies undisturbed by the phantoms of gnawing want. So, in a memorial, "written with tears of blood," as he himself put it, Dee begged the queen to appoint a commission to investigate his case and review the evidence he would produce to prove that his services to the nation warranted a reward. Promptly the commission was appointed, and as promptly began its labors. This led to what Isaac Disraeli, perhaps Dee's best biographer, has described as a "literary scene of singular novelty."

Let me depict it in Disraeli's little known words: "Dee, sitting in his library," says Disraeli, "received the royal commissioners. Two tables were arranged; on one lay all the books he had published, with his unfinished manuscripts; the most extraordinary one was an elaborate narrative of the transactions of his whole life.

This manuscript his secretary read, and, as it proceeded, from the other table Dee presented the commissioners with every testimonial. These vouchers consisted of royal letters from the Queen, and from princes, ambassadors, and the most illustrious persons of England and of Europe; passports which traced his routes, and journals which noted his arrivals and departures; grants and appointments and other remarkable evidences; and when these were wanting, he appealed to living witnesses.

"Among the employments which he had filled, he particularly alluded to a 'painful journey in the winter season, of more than fifteen hundred miles, to confer with learned physicians on the Continent, about her majesty's health.' He showed the offers of many princes to the English philosopher, to retire to their courts, and the princely establishment at Moscow proffered by the czar; but he had never faltered in his devotion to his sovereign.... He complained that his house at Mortlake was too public for his studies, and incommodious for receiving the numerous foreign literati who resorted to him. Of all the promised preferments, he would have chosen the mastership of St. Cross for its seclusion. Here is a great man making great demands, but reposing with dignity on his claims; his wants were urgent, but the penury was not in his spirit. The commissioners, as they listened to his autobiography, must often have raised their eyes in wonder, on the venerable and dignified author before them."

Their report was terse, direct, and wholly favorable, inspiring the queen to declare that Dee should have the mastership of St. Cross, and that immediately. But days passed into months, and months into years, and Elizabeth's "immediately" still belonged to the future. For some reason she soon lost all interest in the returned Sage of Mortlake. Again and again he memorialized her, once with a letter vindicating himself from the accusation of practising sorcery. Her sole reply was to grant him finally the uncongenial post of warden of Manchester College, from which he retired after some mortifying experiences with the minor officials. Nor did he fare better at the hands of Elizabeth's successor. Steadily he sank lower in the scale of society, until at last he was forced to sell his books, one by one, to buy bread. And still, for all his poverty, he pressed constantly forward in his adventurings into the invisible world. If his friends deserted him, he would at least have the companionship of "angels." As his hallucinations grew, his youthful buoyancy returned. He would leave England, would fare across to the Continent, and there seek out men of a mind like unto his own. Joyfully, he made ready for the journey; but, even while he packed and planned, the call came for another and a longer voyage. In the eighty-first year of his age, 1608, the aged dreamer became in very fact a dweller in the spirit world.

Of his place in the history of mankind, it is not easy to write with any degree of finality. There can be no doubt that he was utterly swept off his feet by the domination of a fixed idea. And it is not possible to point to any specific contributions which he made to the advancement of learning, worldly or otherwise. Still, it is equally certain that he was anything but a negative quantity in an age resplendent for its positive men. He played his part, however mistakenly, in the intellectual awakening that has shed such luster on the times of Elizabeth; and, if only for his overpowering curiosity, and his intense and unfailing ardor to get at the truth of all things, natural or supernatural, he merits respect as a forerunner of the scientific spirit which in his day was but feebly striving to loose itself from the bondage of bigotry and intolerance.

XI

GHOST HUNTERS OF YESTERDAY AND TO-DAY

Psychical research, of which so much mention has been made in the preceding pages, may be roughly yet sufficiently described as an effort to determine by strictly scientific methods the nature and significance of apparitions, hauntings, spiritistic phenomena, and those other weird occurrences that would seem to confirm the idea that the spirits of the dead can and do communicate with the living. It is something comparatively new—and like all scientific endeavor is the outgrowth of many minds. But so far as its origin may be attributed to any one man, credit must chiefly be given to a Cambridge University professor named Henry Sidgwick.

At the time, Sidgwick was merely a lecturer in the university, a post given him as a reward for his brilliant career as an undergraduate. He was a born student and investigator, a restless seeker after knowledge. Philosophy, sociology, ethics, economics, mathematics, the classics,—he made almost the whole wide field of thought his sphere of inquiry. And after awhile, as is so often the case, his learning became too profound for his peace of mind. He had been born and brought up in the faith of the English Church, and had unhesitatingly made the religious declaration required of all members of the university faculty. But little by little he felt himself drifting from the moorings of his youth, and doubting the truth of the ancient doctrines and traditions. Honestly skeptical, but still unwilling to lose his hold on religion, he turned feverishly to the study of oriental languages, of ancient philosophies, of history, of science, in the hope of finding evidence that would remove his doubts. But the more he read the greater grew his uncertainty, especially with respect to the vital question of the existence of a spiritual world and its relation to mankind.

While he was still laboring in this valley of indecision, Sidgwick was visited by a young man, Frederic W. H. Myers, who had studied under him a few years earlier and for whom he had formed a warm friendship. Myers, it seemed, was tormented by the same scruples that were harassing him. It was his belief, he told Sidgwick, that if the teachings of the Bible were true—if there existed a spiritual world which in days of old had been manifest to mankind—then such a world should be manifest now. And one beautiful, starlit evening, when they were strolling together through the university grounds, he put to his old master the pointed question:

"Do you think that, although tradition, intuition, metaphysics, have failed to solve the riddle of the universe, there is still a chance of solving it by drawing from actual observable phenomena—ghosts, spirits, whatsoever it may be—valid knowledge as to a world unseen?"

Gazing gravely into the eager face of his companion, and weighing his words with the caution that was characteristic of him, Sidgwick replied that he had indeed entertained this thought; that, although not over hopeful of the result, he believed such an inquiry should be undertaken, notwithstanding the unpleasant notoriety it would entail on those embarking in it. Would he, then, make the quest, and would he permit Myers to pursue it by his side? Long and earnestly the two friends talked together, and when their walk ended, that December night in 1869, psychical research had at last come definitely into being.

In the beginning, however, progress was painfully slow and uncertain. "Our methods," as Myers afterward explained, "were all to make. In those early days we were more devoid of precedents, of guidance, even of criticism that went beyond mere expressions of contempt, than is now readily conceived."

It was realized that no mere analysis of alleged experiences in the past would do; that what was needed was a rigid scrutiny of present-day manifestations of a seemingly supernormal character, and the collection of a mass of well authenticated evidence sufficient to justify inferences and conclusions. Earnestly and bravely the friends went to work, and before long had the satisfaction of finding an invaluable assistant in the person of Edmund Gurney, another Cambridge man and an enthusiast in all matters metaphysical.

At first, to be sure, Gurney entered into psychical research in a half-hearted, quizzical way, expecting to be amused rather than instructed. And he derived little encouragement from the investigations carried on by Sidgwick, Myers, and himself in the field of spiritistic mediumship. Fraud seemed always to be at the bottom of the phenomena produced in the séance room. But his interest was suddenly and permanently awakened by the discovery, following several years spent in patiently collecting evidence, of facts pointing to the possibility of thought being communicated from mind to mind by some agency other than the recognized organs of sense. At once he made it his special business to accumulate data bearing on this point, his labors ultimately leading him into an exhaustive examination of hypnotism, as he found that the hypnotic trance seemed peculiarly favorable to "thought transference," or "telepathy."

Meantime, the example of this little Cambridge group had been followed by other investigators; and in 1876, before no less dignified and conservative a body than the British Association for the Advancement of Science, the proposal was made that a special committee be appointed for the systematic examination of spiritistic and kindred phenomena. The idea was broached by Dr. W. F. Barrett, professor of physics at the Royal College of Science, Dublin, and was warmly seconded by Dr. Alfred Russel Wallace and Sir William Crookes, two distinguished scientists who had already made adventures in psychical research and were destined to wide renown as ghost hunters.

For some reason nothing was done at the time; but five years later Professor Barrett renewed his suggestion, asking Myers and Gurney if they would join him in the formation of such a society. That, they replied, they would gladly do, provided Sidgwick could be induced to accept its presidency. Having long before realized that the field was too extensive for thorough exploration by any individual, however gifted, Sidgwick willingly gave his consent. And accordingly, in January, 1882, the now celebrated Society for Psychical Research was formally organized, its first council including, besides Sidgwick, Myers, Gurney, and Barrett, such men as Arthur J. Balfour, afterward Prime Minister of Great Britain; the brilliant Richard Hutton; Prof. Balfour Stewart; and Frank Podmore, than whom no more merciless executioner of bogus ghosts is wielding the ax to-day.

Unfortunately, the first council also numbered several avowed spiritists, notably the medium Stainton Moses; and the society's birthplace was in the rooms of the British National Association of Spiritualists. These two facts created a wide-spread suspicion that the society was actually nothing more than an adjunct to the spiritistic movement. Nor was confidence wholly restored by the hasty withdrawal of the spiritistic representatives as soon as they learned that strictly scientific methods of inquiry were to prevail; or by the accession, as honorary members, of national figures like W. E. Gladstone, John Ruskin, Lord Tennyson, A. R. Wallace, Sir William Crookes, and G. F. Watts.

To the scientific as well as the popular consciousness, the society was little better than an assemblage of cranks, with strangely fantastic notions, and only too likely to lose its mental balance and help ignorant and superstitious people to lose theirs. Conscious, however, of the really serious and important nature of their enterprise, and cheered by Gladstone's comforting assurance that no investigation of greater moment to mankind could be made, the members of the society applied themselves zealously to the business that had brought them together.

Sensibly enough, they adopted the principle of specialization and division of labor. While one group carried on experiments designed to prove or disprove the telepathic hypothesis, another engaged in a systematic examination of the alleged facts of clairvoyance. A third, in its turn, under the skilful guidance of Gurney, investigated the phenomena of the hypnotic trance, with results unexpectedly beneficial to medical science. A special committee was also appointed to collect and sift evidence as to the reality of apparitions and hauntings, making whenever possible personal examinations of the seers of the visions and the places of their occurrence. Finally, there were various subcommittees of inquiry into the physical phenomena of spiritism,—the knockings, table turnings, production of spirit forms, and similar marvels of the Dunglas Home type of "medium." From the outset, these subcommittees demonstrated the value of psychical research, as a protection to the interests of society, by exposing, one after another, the fraudulent character of the pretended intermediaries between the seen and the unseen world.

In this region of inquiry no one was more successful than a recruit from distant Australia, by name Richard Hodgson. Hodgson, unlike Sidgwick and Myers and many others of his associates, had not engaged in psychical research from the hope that the truths of the Bible might thereby be demonstrated. His motive was that of the detective eager to unravel mysteries. From his boyhood he had had a singular fondness for solving tricks and puzzles of all sorts; and when, in 1878, he came to England to complete his education at Cambridge, he naturally gravitated into the company of Sidgwick, Myers, and Gurney, as men busied in an undertaking that appealed to his detective instinct. He was radically different from them in temperament and point of view—not at all mystical, full of animal spirits, fond of all manner of sports, and interested in occult subjects only so far as they furnished working material for his nimble and inquiring mind. The Cambridge trio, however, took kindly to him, invited him to join the Society for Psychical Research, and two years after its formation were instrumental in sending him to India to investigate the methods of Madam Blavatsky, the high priestess of the theosophic movement which was then winning adherents throughout the civilized world.

From this inquiry he returned to England with an international reputation as a detective of the supernatural. With the aid of two disgruntled confederates of the theosophist leader, he had demonstrated the falsity of the foundations on which her claims rested, and had shown that downright swindling constituted a large part of her stock in trade. With redoubled ardor he now plunged into the task of exposing the spiritistic mediums plying their vocation in England, and for this purpose enlisted the assistance of a professional conjurer, S. J. Davey, who was also a member of the Society for Psychical Research.

Davey, after a little practice, succeeded in duplicating by mere sleight of hand many of the most impressive feats of the mediums; doing this, indeed, so well that some spiritists alleged that he was in reality a medium himself. Hodgson, for his part, by clever analysis of the Davey performances and of the feats of Davey's mediumistic competitors, brought home to his colleagues in the Society for Psychical Research a lively sense of the folly of depending on the human eye as a detector of fraudulent spiritistic phenomena. His crowning triumph came with his exposure of Eusapia Paladino, the Italian medium who is still enjoying an undeserved popularity on the European continent.

But in time even Hodgson met his Waterloo. Sent to the United States to investigate the trance phenomena of Mrs. Leonora Piper, he was forced to confess that in her case the theory of fraud fell to the ground, and as is well known he ended by developing into an out and out spiritist. A few days before Christmas, 1905, he suddenly died in Boston; and, if reports from the spirit world may be accepted, the once-renowned ghost hunter has himself become a ghost, visiting in especial two of his American colleagues, Prof. William James and Prof. James H. Hyslop.

To return, however, to the early days of the Society for Psychical Research. Valuable as were the results obtained by Hodgson and his associates on what may be called the anti-swindle committees, they had a distinctly negative bearing on the supreme object of inquiry—proof of the existence of a spiritual world in which human personality exists after the death of the body. Some enthusiasts did not hesitate to proclaim at an early date that such proof had actually been secured, basing this assertion on the seemingly supernatural facts brought to light by the committees on telepathy, clairvoyance, and apparitions. But the society, under the leadership of the cautious Sidgwick, who was its president for many years, steadily refused to countenance this view, and insisted that before any definite conclusions could be reached far more evidence would have to be assembled. Thus the first ten years of the society's existence were marked by few positive results,—the most important being the statement of the case for telepathy and of its possible relationships to apparitions and hauntings, as well as to the purely psychical phenomena of spiritualism.

Indeed, the society formally expressed its acquiescence in the telepathic hypothesis as early as 1884, in the words, "Our society claims to have proved the reality of thought transference—of the transmission of thoughts, feelings, and images from one mind to another by no recognized channel of sense." But to no other dictum did it commit itself until ten years more had passed when, following the so-called census of hallucinations, it gave voice to its belief that between deaths and apparitions of the dying person a connection existed that was not due to chance. And since then the society has contented itself with steadily accumulating evidence designed to throw light on the causal connection between deaths and ghosts, and to illumine the central problem of demonstrating scientifically the existence of an unseen world and the immortality of the soul.

Individuals, of course, have been free to express their views, and from the pens of several have come striking and suggestive analyses of the evidence assembled in the course of the society's twenty-five years. In this respect, beyond any question, primacy must be given the writings of Myers. Even before the organization of the society, his personal researches had led him to suspect that, whatever the truth about the life beyond the grave, there was reason for radical changes of belief regarding the nature of human personality itself. In the light of the phenomena of the hypnotic trance, clairvoyance, hallucinations, and even of natural sleep, it seemed to him that, instead of being a stable, indivisible unity, human personality was essentially unstable and divisible.

And as the years passed and he was enabled to coördinate the results of the investigations carried on by the different committees, he gradually became convinced that over and beyond the self of which man is normally conscious there existed in every man a secondary self endowed with faculties transcending those of the normal wake-a-day self. To this he gave the name of the "subliminal self," and, in the words of Professor James, "endowed psychology with a new problem,—the exploration of the subliminal region being destined to figure thereafter in that branch of learning as Myers's problem."

Not content with this, he gave himself, with all the earnestness that had originally drawn him into activity with Sidgwick, to the formulation of a cosmic philosophy based on the hypothesis of the subliminal self and its operations in that unseen world of whose existence he no longer doubted. Here he laid himself open to the charge of extravagance and transcendentalism, and undoubtedly exceeded the logical limit. But for all of that his labors—cut short by death six years ago, and only a few months after the death of his beloved master,

Sidgwick—have been little short of epoch marking, and amply suffice to vindicate the existence of the once despised, and still by no means venerated, Society for Psychical Research.

Sir William Crookes, Sir Oliver Lodge, and Mr. Frank Podmore are other members of the society who have granted the outside world informative glimpses of its workings and discoveries. Sir William Crookes, of course, is best known as a great chemist, discoverer of the element thallium, and inventor of numerous scientific instruments; while Sir Oliver Lodge's most striking work has been in electricity, and more particularly in the direction of improving wireless telegraphy. But both have long been actively interested in psychical research, and perhaps most of all in those phases of it bearing on the telepathic hypothesis, their great aim being to discover just what the technique of telepathic communication from mind to mind may be.

Mr. Podmore, on the other hand, like Richard Hodgson, has chiefly concerned himself with psychical research from the detective, or critical, standpoint. He began his labors late in the '70's, associating himself with the Cambridge group, and has consistently maintained the attitude of a skeptical, though open minded, investigator. To-day, to a certain extent, he may be said to occupy the place so long filled by Henry Sidgwick as a sane, restraining influence on the less judicial members of the society, who would unhesitatingly brush aside all objections and embrace the spiritistic hypothesis with all its supernatural implications.

Of course, psychical research has by no means been confined to the English organization. All over the world investigators are now probing into the mysteries of the seemingly supernormal. But, as a general thing, their methods scarcely reach the strict standards set by the organized inquirers of England, and as a natural consequence they are more easily deceived by tricksters.

This is particularly true of the European ghost hunters, whose laxity of procedure, not to say gullibility, was clearly shown by the ease with which Hodgson exposed the pretensions of Eusapia Paladino after Continental savants had pronounced her feats genuine. And it is even more strikingly exhibited by the pathetic fidelity with which they still trust in her, notwithstanding the Hodgson exposure, and the fact that they themselves have on more than one occasion caught her committing fraud. In the United States, however, psychical research worthy of the name took root early, owing to the establishment of an American branch of the English society under the capable direction of Dr. Hodgson. A year or so ago, after his death, this branch was abandoned. But in its place, and organized along similar lines, there has arisen the American Institute for Scientific Research, the creation of Prof. James H. Hyslop.

Until a few years ago occupant of the chair of logic at Columbia University, Professor Hyslop is unquestionably one of the most conspicuous figures in psychical research in this or any other country. Like Professor Sidgwick, he first became interested in the subject through religious doubt, and forthwith attacked its problems with the zeal of a man whose principal characteristics are intense enthusiasm, resourcefulness of wit, and intellectual fearlessness. As everybody knows, his experiences with Mrs. Piper led him to unite with Hodgson and Myers in regarding the spiritistic hypothesis as the only one capable of explaining all the phenomena encountered. But he is none the less able and eager to expose fraud wherever found, and if only from the police view-point his society will undoubtedly do good work. Associated with him are many of the American investigators formerly identified with the English society; some of whom, notably Prof. William James of Harvard, the dean of psychical research in the United States, also keep up their connection with the parent organization.

Summing up the results of the really scientific ghost hunting of the last twenty-five years, it may be safely said that if the hunters have not accomplished their main object of definitely proving the existence of a spiritual world, their labors have nevertheless been of high value in several important directions. They have exposed the fraudulent pretensions of innumerable charlatans, and have thus acted as a protection for the credulous. They have shown that, making all possible allowance for error of whatever kind, there still remains in the phenomena of apparitions, clairvoyance, etc., a residuum not explainable on the hypothesis of fraud or chance coincidence. They have aided in giving validity to the idea of the influence of suggestion as a factor both in the cause and the cure of disease. They have given a needed stimulus to the study of abnormal mental conditions. And, finally, by the discovery of the impressive facts that led Myers to formulate his hypothesis of the subliminal self, they have opened the door to far-reaching reforms in the whole sociological domain,—in education, in the treatment of vice and crime, in all else that makes for the uplifting of the human race.

Echo Library
www.echo-library.com

Echo Library uses advanced digital print-on-demand technology to build and preserve an exciting world class collection of rare and out-of-print books, making them readily available for everyone to enjoy.

Situated just yards from Teddington Lock on the River Thames, Echo Library was founded in 2005 by Tom Cherrington, a specialist dealer in rare and antiquarian books with a passion for literature.

Please visit our website for a complete catalogue of our books, which includes foreign language titles.

The Right to Read
Echo Library actively supports the Royal National Institute of the Blind's Right to Read initiative by publishing a comprehensive range of large print and clear print titles.

Large Print titles are in 16 point Tiresias font as recommended by the RNIB.

Clear Print titles are in 13 point Tiresias font and designed for those who find standard print difficult to read.

Customer Service
If there is a serious error in the text or layout please send details to feedback@echo-library.com and we will supply a corrected copy. If there is a printing fault or the book is damaged please refer to your supplier.

Lightning Source UK Ltd.
Milton Keynes UK
UKOW051503230712

196440UK00002B/183/P